WILD RIVERS OF ALASKA

WILD RIVERS
OF ALASKA
Sepp Weber

ALASKA NORTHWEST PUBLISHING COMPANY
Anchorage, Alaska

Cover—*Flora Creek, a stream c
the headwaters of the Aniuk
River in the Brooks Range, is th
starting point of a voyage
southwest to the Noatak River
and Kotzebue Sound on the
Chukchi Sea* (*see pages
143 and 149*).
Frontispiece—*Loading the kaya
before setting out on the
Tikchik River.*
Overleaf—*Kayakers set out on
a voyage down the Nigu River
from its headwaters in the
Brooks Range.*
Below—*Launching collapsible
kayaks on the Aniuk River fror
a bank covered with cotton grass*

First printing October 1976
Second printing May 1977

Library of Congress cataloging in publication data:
Weber, Sepp, 1929-
    Wild rivers of Alaska.
    Includes index.
    1. Alaska—Description and travel—1959-
—Guide-books. 2. Wild and scenic rivers—Alaska.
I. Title.
F902.3.W42   917.98'04'5   76-15272
ISBN 0-88240-071-1

Design by Dianne Hofbeck
CartoGraphics by Jon.Hersh
Alaska Northwest Publishing Company
Box 4-EEE, Anchorage, Alaska 99509

Printed in U.S.A.

Contents

Introduction   1

THE RIVERS OF ALASKA   2
Truly Wild   4
Where Rivers Flow   6
Conservation or Development?   10
History of River Exploration   14
People on the Rivers   16
River Chronicles   20
    The Noatak River—Arctic Beauty   22
    The Aniak—River of the Bears   29
    The Porcupine River—Hudson's Bay Company Fur Route   34
    The Copper River—Violent Performance at Breakup   38
    The Chilikadrotna—Fast River Through the Forest   42

VOYAGING THE WILD RIVERS   44
Choosing a Craft   46
Preparation and Equipment   49
Transportation   49
Challenge and Ability   50
Judging Objectively   54
Evaluating the Rivers   55
    White-Water Classifications   58
    Craft Classifications   59
    Flat-Water Classifications   59

FIFTY-THREE RIVERS   60
    Please see index for alphabetical listing of rivers.

Index   168

Dedicated to Brigitte and Arno

Introduction

On every continent rivers call men out of their safe, comfortable homes and cause them to live in simple tents, sleep on hard ground, endure hardships and frequently face extraordinary risks. While there are no truly new rivers to discover, the persistent challenge of flowing water attracts growing numbers of travelers seeking the subtle rewards of a placid stream or the high adventure of frothing white water.

As a little boy, I spent hours on the banks of a small stream that, in reality, was just a trickle. It was the focal point of my daydreams; it represented the thrill of adventure, of voyages down to the distant sea. Recently, I returned to the place of my childhood. The houses were still there, the people and the mountains. But the picture was flawed, something missing. My little stream was gone, a victim of progress. The horse-drawn wagons of my childhood had given way to tractors. The road had been widened to accommodate them, and in the process the "useless" little stream was filled in.

Now my young son has discovered his own small stream. Day after day he drags me there to watch water rush by, as he sends tiny sticks down to the ocean. Will he someday return to the place of his childhood and find the stream missing? I hope not. Fortunately, our home is Alaska, and its remoteness seems to insulate us from some forms of "progress." Besides, all the nation's waters are now more important, and there's a strong and growing awareness that they should be protected and preserved. People are flocking to the rivers and streams in ever-increasing numbers for rafting, canoeing and kayaking. More and more people are looking to Alaska as the place where childhood dreams of adventure on uncrowded waterways can come true.

This book's aim is to stimulate prospective voyagers and to give substance to the dreams of vicarious travelers. But given the vast dimensions of Alaska's wild rivers, I can do no more than offer a broad picture, leaving blank spaces that must be filled with a stroke of the paddle or a flight of imagination.

I write this book with mixed emotions. Like many others, I came to Alaska because of its vastness, its solitude, its delights. By sharing what I have discovered, more people will be attracted to "my" places. But there's no real reason to be stingy. After all, there are countless Alaskan rivers and streams to reexplore. From the beginning, men have been sharing them—Indians and Eskimos, trappers and prospectors, Russians and Englishmen.

Now there may be no rivers or streams that have escaped the tread of human feet along their banks or felt the soft stroke of paddles on their surfaces. Yet the waters remain unmarked and that's the magic of it all. Sometimes a cut, rotten old log or perhaps a few blackened campfire rocks show someone's passed. Often there is nothing but the water and the shore. I like it this way. I've come to enjoy, to meet the challenge and to explore. And I leave the river as I found it, taking with me a memory of solitude, rushing waters, a cloudburst and sometimes a howl from a lone wolf. If I can show others the way to these treasures, and they come to respect them as I do, I will be content.

Left—Sepp and Brigitte Weber paddling the Chilikadrotna, one of their many voyages together on Alaska's wild rivers.

THE RIVERS OF
ALASKA

Truly Wild

Thoughts of wild rivers conjure up visions of running water, sheer-walled canyons and thundering waterfalls. But wild really means a sense of being untamed, unadulterated—a place where nature and animals are in harmonious balance, where man is a visitor, an intruder. Almost all Alaskan rivers are wild in this sense. This is their great attraction and creates their great challenge.

A wild river can be a mountain torrent or a broad stream flowing through an open valley. The character of each varies with the major source of its waters and the terrain through which it flows. Rain, snowfall, glaciers, muskegs and lakes combine with temperature to contribute to the

Overleaf—*Mount Deborah and Mount Hayes in the Alaska Range as seen from the upper Susitna River.*
Below—*A wild river in Arctic Alaska.*

river's water volume, its velocity and its purity. Geological features determine current, the location of rapids and the course of the riverbed.

Almost all Alaskan rivers may be negotiated by small boats, but at times some pose risks even beyond the skill of the most experienced boatman. Compounding the challenge is the fact that conditions can change daily, often by the hour. What once was a placid river can turn into a hellish nightmare of foaming water. Other rivers may dry up quickly to rocky roads that will not float a boat. Rivers that are run in different years, at the same time of the year, can change beyond recognition.

This is the challenge: The rivers are unpredictable. A voyager must depend on his own skill and resources. Planning, common sense, skill and expertise on the water are musts to successfully challenging the remote back country surrounding Alaska's rivers—all of them truly wild.

Where Rivers Flow

Arctic Oc

Chukchi Sea

De Long Mtns.

Brooks **Rang**

Noatak River

Baird Mtns.

Endicott Mtns.

Kobuk River

Po

Koyukuk River

Yukon River

Fairbanks

Tanana

Bering Sea

Kuskokwim River

Alaska Range

River

Susitna

Talkeetna Mtns.

Anchorage **Chugach**

Nushagak River

Aleutian Range

Kenai Mtns.

Gulf of Alask

The mountain ranges in Alaska arch across the state from east to west. Farthest north is the Brooks Range, a geologically old, upfolded group of mountains greatly eroded and furrowed by many swift rivers. North of this range, streams pierce the arctic foothills to join rivers that empty into the Arctic Ocean. The flat coastal plains are dotted with ponds, lakes and lagoons. The forested forelands south of the Brooks Range are drained by southerly flowing rivers that eventually swing westward to reach the Bering Sea. Many streams and rivers join the Porcupine and Koyukuk, rivers whose waters flow into the mighty Yukon River.

Two major rivers in the Brooks Range flow directly west. To the north, the Noatak, a clear gravelly river, meanders between the DeLong and Baird Mountains. Its headwaters drain portions of the Endicott Mountains. The greater part of the Noatak flows through tundra country, but after cutting through Noatak Canyon, it traverses a forested region before emptying into Kotzebue Sound. South of the Noatak, the Kobuk River skirts the mountains and flows placidly through the forest, also toward Kotzebue Sound. It enters salt water a few miles south of the mouth of the Noatak.

The Alaska Range reaches 650 miles across southern Alaska toward the lower Aleutian Range in the west. The highest point in North America, 20,320-foot Mount McKinley, dominates the Alaska Range. Rivers spawned by the glaciers on

Alsek River

Taku River

Stikine River

Mtns.

Coast Mtns.

Juneau•

Wrangell•

the slopes of this mountain range flow north, south and west to merge eventually with the Tanana, Susitna and Kuskokwim rivers.

Between the Alaska and Brooks ranges sprawls Alaska's vast Interior, an area drained by the Yukon and Kuskokwim rivers in their drive to the Bering Sea. Thousands of lesser streams crisscross the hills and valleys of the Interior. The myriad streams and rivers range from deep, narrow creeks flowing through muskeg to clear, cascading mountain rivers. Enormous meanders, island-dotted courses and deep canyons mark the course of the major rivers on their way to the sea.

The Saint Elias, Chugach and Kenai Mountains stretch along the coast of the Gulf of Alaska. The Wrangell and Talkeetna Mountains lie farther north. An obvious scenic feature of the whole coastal range is the extensive glaciation. The silty, ice-cold rivers of this region are short and have violent descents. Their rapids and stark scenic beauty exert strong attractions to wilderness voyagers. However, the glacial rivers in the coastal range are, with few exceptions, only for well-trained, well-equipped, expert paddlers. The Aleutian Range, to the west, produces its own unique rivers, sending them along short, swift courses to the Pacific Ocean or the Bering Sea.

Between the coastal mountains and the Alaska Range, some extensive lowland areas hold a host of lakes. Many rivers rise here and work their way to the Copper River basin, to the Susitna Valley or to the Nushagak

The Noatak River.

Valley, west of the Aleutian Range. These streams frequently originate in deep, clear lakes and flow swiftly through coniferous and deciduous forests, also passing at times through muskeg flats. Along the way they occasionally offer spectacular waterfalls and rapids.

The narrow coastal strip that is Alaska's Panhandle is known for its fractured coastline, steep mountains and a series of offshore islands that create protected inland passages. Three major rivers push through the mountains to the sea in this area: the Stikine at Wrangell; the Taku at Juneau; and the Alsek at Dry Bay. The Alsek deserves special mention. Although most of its course runs through Canada, its water volume is second only to that of the Columbia in the Pacific Northwest. For grandeur the Alsek is unmatched, cutting through glaciers as it forces its way through 10,000-foot-high mountains in its race to the Gulf of Alaska. It has been called "Alaska's unrunable river."

Alaska's wild rivers are produced by a country that creates each one with a difference that can satisfy thousands of river enthusiasts—the careful and patient person, the strong challenger and, above all, the casual voyager who comes to explore his own limit of solitude and endurance. In the process, each voyager may take some unforgettable memory back to those places where small streams or wild rivers have been destroyed.

Conservation or Development?

For thousands of years, Natives hunted, fished and set up camps on the banks of Alaska's rivers without altering them; the rivers remained virtually untouched. More recently, explorers used these same rivers as routes to the Interior, founding villages and towns along the way, and still the rivers did not change much. Some rivers now are spanned by bridges. A few more are touched by roads. A handful are used as garbage dumps by villages or towns, and a small number of creeks are so polluted that they are unfit for any recreational use. But, by and large, most Alaskan rivers remain wild.

Hydroelectric power developers are taking a new look at Alaska's rivers as potential power suppliers. The Susitna River at Devil Canyon seems destined to become the first major Alaskan river to be dammed. Other hydroelectric projects may follow in keeping with the state's population

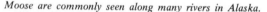

Moose are commonly seen along many rivers in Alaska.

Fish wheel on the Copper River.

growth forecast. Alaska, with its 10,000 rivers and streams, can set aside a few for development of hydroelectric power plants. But, equally, many should be set aside for recreational use, and a score could be set aside as wilderness areas.

A significant step toward preserving some rivers was taken by the U.S. Congress with passage of the Wild and Scenic Rivers Act, Public Law 90-542, in 1968. Of approximately 365,000 miles of rivers in Alaska, federal and state agencies and conservation groups have recommended that 166 rivers, totaling about 15,000 miles, be included in the system. Of these, 69 rivers, totaling approximately 7,000 miles, have been surveyed by aerial reconnaissance and are under active consideration. Virtually all Alaskan rivers could meet the criteria needed for them to be included in the National Wild and Scenic Rivers System; 69 out of 10,000 does not seem extravagant.

Clockwise from right—
*Modern-day explorers camp on the
gravelly banks of a river in the
Alaskan wilderness.
Waking up with ice-cold water
from the river.
Picking blueberries on a hill above
the Aniuk River, a pleasant diversion
after a day's paddling.
Fresh fish bring a welcome call to supper.
A needed rest before the next day's
challenge, a portage around the waterfall.*

History Of River Exploration

Eskimos hunting from kayaks return from the Arctic Coast with ringed seal.

Exploration of Interior Alaska is a story of river navigation. Natives, of course, have known the rivers for thousands of years and used them as a means of transportation and a source of food. Russian navigators slowly penetrated the Interior. Their main economic interest always had been the coastal sea otters. Besides, they lacked the means to ascend swift and intricate waterways. Their heavy, clumsy skin boats did not lend themselves to inland river travel where portages and upriver travel are necessary.

It was not until 1818 that the first significant penetration of the Interior occurred. Korasakovsky explored the southwestern part of the region by boat on a voyage from Cook Inlet to Iliamna Lake, and thence to Bristol Bay. He continued north to the mouth of the Nushagak River, then around Cape Newenham finally reaching the wide estuary of the Kuskokwim River. A year later, Klimowski ascended the Copper River to the mouth of the Chitina River, possibly even traveling up to the Gulkana River.

Records are unclear, but hostility of the local Indians apparently forced successive attempts to ascend the Copper River to be unsuccessful.

Ten years later, in 1829, a Russian party headed by Vasilief traveled up the Nushagak River from Bristol Bay to the Tikchik Lakes, portaged to the Holitna River and went down it to the Kuskokwim River and the coast where the Russian-American Company had a trading post. They returned to Bristol Bay the same year along the Arctic Coast. Another Russian, A. Kolmakof, ascended the Kuskokwim to the Takotna River in the same year. The largest river, the Yukon, was navigated in 1838 to its mouth by Malakof after he explored the Koyukuk River. Malakof did not attempt the swift channels of the expansive Yukon Delta.

The Russians established a trading post at Nulato, trading with Indians as far inland as the Tanana. About the same time, the Hudson's Bay Company established a trading post at the confluence of the Porcupine and Yukon rivers, Fort Yukon. The Russians and English never established contact directly although they knew of each other's activities.

Before the purchase of Alaska by the United States in 1867, there were additional attempts to penetrate the Interior. One party of 13 set out to ascend the swift Copper River but disappeared. Indian stories put them as far north as the Fortymile River, a tributary of the Yukon. A portage from the Yukon to the Kuskokwim was blazed in 1834 by Glazanof. The Kuskokwim was ascended, possibly as far as Stony River and Lime Hills.

After the time of the purchase of Russian America by the United States, the Interior remained virtually untouched until the discovery of gold touched off a general demand for accurate maps and information. In response, the government sent out survey and scientific parties. Lt. G. M. Stoney and John C. Cantwell explored the Kobuk River Valley to its source in two different expeditions between 1884 and 1886. They used gas boats as far up the river as the village of Kobuk, 250 miles from the ocean, then converted to canoes to reach Walker Lake.

The year of the big Klondike strike saw the Glenn expedition ascending the fast Matanuska River and then portaging to the Copper River basin. After reaching the headwaters of the Delta River, they descended to the Tanana River. These early explorers' journeys, which today seem incredible, were accomplished without accurate maps or good equipment, and helped push back the borders of then unknown Interior Alaska.

People on the Rivers

With the end of the last ice age, continental Indians pushed north, eventually forcing the Eskimos out of Interior Alaska and into coastal areas. In all likelihood, migration routes followed major valleys, waterways and plains. These same routes later became avenues of trade. A few isolated bands of inland Eskimos depended on caribou for food and became great travelers out of necessity, as they chased the wandering herds. In late spring, for example, Eskimo families traveled up the Ambler and Redstone rivers to low passes where they hunted caribou. Making boats of wooden frames and animal skins, they floated the Noatak River to Kotzebue Sound. After trading with coastal Eskimos, these people again headed up the Kobuk River, now to fish for salmon.

One summer, I retraced this route and found signs of the early travelers: rows of rock cairns used for funneling the caribou into hunting corrals, tent rings built of stone and a burial site. Robert Cleveland, an elderly Eskimo who had covered the route as a child, drew a map to guide me to a mountain hot spring used regularly by early Eskimos. I found the spring easily and tested its medicinal properties.

As recently as the late 1940's, the Anaktuvuk Eskimos were nomadic, roaming in small bands over the central and western Brooks Range in search of the wandering caribou. Anaktuvuk Pass, in the central Brooks Range, was just one of their favorite hunting grounds, but it became a winter settlement, because large bands of caribou came through the pass at the beginning of winter. There was contact between the Koyukuk Indians and the Anaktuvuk Eskimos, but the meetings were not always friendly. Stories about war parties still circulate among the people.

Tracing the historic path of these inland Eskimos, I once traveled north up the John River Valley to Anaktuvuk Pass, over the Brooks Range and down the swift Anaktuvuk River to the Colville River, then west along the Arctic Coast to Point Barrow. Foldboats and lightweight equipment made it a relatively easy journey. In the early 1930's, however, a trader lined a bulky, 1-ton wooden boat loaded with trading supplies up the John River from Bettles to Anaktuvuk Pass. He then dragged the boat 20 miles across the pass, descended the Anaktuvuk River to the Colville River delta and established a trading post.

In the early fur trading days, the Hudson's Bay Company moved freight from the Mackenzie River to the Yukon River by the way of the Rat, Bell

Right—*Brigitte examines a new handmade canoe along the Nushagak River.*

and Porcupine rivers. Old Crow on the Porcupine is now the only settlement along the route, but then there were many inhabited places, such as LaPierre House on the upper Bell and Old Rampart and Rampart House below Old Crow. I have met some remarkable people along this old fur route. One, a young Canadian whose path crossed mine while he was on a long voyage to the Mạckenzie delta, wanted to join me on my last leg of a trip along the Porcupine fur route to the Yukon. We agreed, but somehow we later missed our rendezvous, and I continued alone.

Fall was in the air, so I paddled well into the evenings. At dusk on the fourth day, I caught up with two Indians who were floating on a raft of firewood to Old Crow. Caribou were traveling along the river, and they had shot a dozen and loaded them onto the raft. A tent also was pitched on the raft. I spent the rest of the evening very pleasantly feasting on caribou heart and tongue, my kayak riding on the front section of the raft with the caribou carcasses.

In the dark of the night, a sudden jolt awoke me. We had rammed a large boulder. The raft broke into three parts; the first section with the caribou and my kayak disappeared around a corner. It took us the rest of the night to free our section and get it floating again. We caught up with the runaway section at Old Crow where the people had retrieved it as it drifted by.

Several weeks later back in Anchorage, I had all but forgotten about the young Canadian when I got a letter from a hospital in Inuvik, a town on the delta of the Mackenzie River. The Canadian reported that, while making the trip alone, he capsized his open canoe on the Little Bell River and lost all his gear. He managed to subsist on berries for 4 weeks until a plane spotted him, and he was rescued. He had lost 50 of his 130 pounds and considered himself very lucky to have survived.

Some of the old Indian travel routes are still in use, as I learned a few summers ago on the upper Yukon. That afternoon, while paddling below the Little Salmon River, I saw smoke rising through the trees and stopped to investigate. There stood an old cabin without doors or windows and with a fire for smoking burning in the clearing before it. Freshly killed moose meat was hanging there to dry. On the bank was a log raft of a very delicate design. The owners, two men and two women, were drifting downriver hunting beaver.

People did not travel the entire length of the fierce Alsek River until 1961. The Russians discovered the river, which enters the Gulf of Alaska at Dry Bay, in the early 1800's, but it was so violent and formidable that they never attempted to ascend it. Upstream portions, however, were used by prospectors in 1898 and the early 20th century. The Alsek was run for the first time all the way to its mouth in 1961 by two paddlers from

A Noatak boy (left), although shy of the camera, proudly shows off his self-made kayak. Charley Peters (right) of Old Crow.

Fairbanks, Clem Rawert and John Dawson. They started at Haines Junction and in 3 weeks paddled to Dry Bay in the Gulf of Alaska. The trip included a 10-mile portage across Tweedsmuir Glacier to skirt the unnavigable Turnback Canyon.

Ten years later, a 49-year-old physician from Salmon, Idaho, Dr. Walt Blackadar, did paddle Turnback Canyon in a single kayak. It was a foolhardy feat. Dr. Blackadar concedes that the canyon is unpaddleable. Now, even the route over Tweedsmuir Glacier is not passable, a surge sometime in 1974 having jumbled the glacier. It may take years before the Alsek can be traversed again.

Many voyagers have come and gone. One voyager has come and stayed, running Alaska's rivers for the last 30 years. A legend already, Charlie Wolf of Fairbanks has traveled tens of thousands of miles on the rivers between the Bering Sea and Hudson Bay. In 1975, I finally managed to meet him and his wife, just as he was setting out for another one of his long voyages. Paddling a 14-foot aluminum canoe, self-sufficient and independent, every summer Wolf, now more than 70, is testing some northern river.

River Chronicles

No two rivers are totally alike, for each is subject to a variety of moods that always are changing. As an aid to recalling the subtleties of a certain river on a particular voyage, I have made it a practice to take notes as I travel. When possible, I also take pictures, so that my wife, Brigitte, who accompanies me on many trips, and I can return again, and again, to the experiences of a special time out of doors.

Trees again after days of travel through the tundra country of the Noatak River.

I have chosen notes from five rivers—the Noatak, the Aniak, the Porcupine, the Copper and the Chilikadrotna—for inclusion in this book because these rivers generally are typical of the streams in their respective regions. Some of them I have traveled often. No two voyages ever will be totally alike, but this sampling can give prospective voyagers a foretaste of what they might expect from a variety of wild rivers.

The Noatak River
Arctic Beauty

The Noatak River is truly an arctic river, for all of its 425 miles are north of the Arctic Circle. Only one settlement, Noatak, 60 miles from its mouth, lies along its banks. Crystal clear, except for its last 100 miles, it follows a graceful, sweeping arc westward. Deflected gently to the south along the De Long Mountains, it enters Kotzebue Sound only some 30 miles from the Kobuk River.

From a low in April of 120 cubic feet per second, the Noatak rises to a high of as much as 240,000 cubic feet per second in June. On any given summer day, its flow may triple or drop by two-thirds. The entire length of the Noatak is navigable in season.

The Noatak River is Eskimo country. For centuries before permanent settlements were established, the people roamed the western Brooks Range in search of the ever-shifting caribou. They discovered, and used, the Koyukuk and Alatna valleys by way of Portage Creek near the headwaters of the Noatak.

The river pierces a region where there are sheep, goats, caribou, black and grizzly bear, wolf and moose. Salmon ascend the river,

Right—The Noatak is deflected gently south along the De Long Mountains.

Above—*The Noatak occasionally braids into several channels.* Right—*Permafrost exposed on the bank of the Noatak.*

A pause for fishing and Sepp makes a catch, a nice salmon.

and some sheefish and an abundance of grayling are found in its clear waters.

The sound faded even before the small plane dissolved into the uniform pale blue of the sky. Surrounded by a pile of gear, we viewed the river that was to be our temporary home. It had seen many travelers, yet it still conveyed a strong feeling of remoteness.

Later, with our heavily loaded boats packed with provisions and camping gear for 3 weeks, we entered the current and drifted lazily along the meandering stream. It flows through a wide valley among old, well-worn mountains that are set back, letting the eyes roam freely. Over the years, the river has shifted its bed back and forth across the valley and created countless lakes and ponds where birds now nest.

Much later after making camp and retiring to our tent, we watched mosquitoes dance in the bright sun in front of our mosquito netting. At ten in the evening there was still no

hint of darkness. It was utterly quiet. The call of a loon from a nearby lake floated through the stillness.

Occasionally the river flexes its muscle by braiding into several channels, creating riffles and shallows where our canoe scraped bottom. At times we had to jump out to get the canoe floating again. We set up camp where the valley ahead opened up. The tent pitched, food stashed and boat secured, we set out to climb a mountain. The sun dipped toward the north as we crested the last rise. To the east we saw a sea of mountains. To the north and west lay rolling hills and plains dotted with shiny ponds. The river below was a strand of gold.

The next day, we passed Midas Creek, another route once used as a pass by the Eskimos. The Natives had followed the creek to reach the Ambler River, and eventually the Kobuk, where they had opportunity to trade for goods from distant Siberia.

We met a prospector heading for his claim on the upper Noatak to work it over the summer as was his habit. He didn't need to work. He owns several valuable jade claims on the Kobuk, and gossip said that he sold a huge copper claim for tens of thousands of dollars. But there he was, all by himself, as always.

Gradually, the mountains fell behind us and the tundra took over. A major tributary, the Aniuk River, rippled over the clean gravel bar signaling the end of a very long day of paddling. As the shadows grew longer, a cool breeze from the north encouraged a blazing campfire. In the middle of a sunlit night, a wolf howled and was answered.

Another bright day dawned. Drifting along the high banks we were startled as a caribou suddenly jumped up from its slumber on the sunny bank. All day, bull caribou moved along the river. One carcass deteriorated in the heat of the day, swarms of flies blackening it where the wolves had eaten. We made a camp stop on the Cutler River, another route of early travelers between the Kobuk and the Noatak rivers. A wolf trotted along the bank, and a fox appeared. We still saw caribou.

At another campsite we found a ring of rocks overgrown with moss marking the spot where a skin tent had stood many years ago. The weather was holding and the water level dropping, but the Nimiuktuk River was feeding in muddy water, indicating that there were showers in the mountains.

After a week of travel, the first spruce trees pierced the flat horizon. It was a pleasure to zero in on a definite object again instead of visually sweeping an unbroken expanse of tundra. Out of the haze, mountains appeared and a V-shaped opening marked the beginning of the grand canyon of the Noatak. Clouds were building up, then rain started to fall. Nowhere was the river difficult;

however, there were many passages and chutes with 2- to 3-foot-high standing waves. Rocky cliffs and boulders narrowed the riverbed and quickened the waters. We discovered a good campsite before leaving the mountains.

Next morning we found rushing water where the boat had been moored. Luckily, we located it 3 miles downstream, hung up on a rock. Rain had raised the water level 5 feet overnight taking our beached, but not tied, canoe with it. It was a lesson we didn't forget.

Under way again, the tundra hesitantly gave way more and more to trees and forest. A porcupine swam across the river and hitched a ride with us. A clear water slough encouraged us to stop for the night, providing grayling and salmon for our supper.

The hum of a generator early the next day announced the village of Noatak. Houses were strung out along the banks. There was a store,

Above—*A porcupine hitches a ride on the kayak.*
Left—*White water on the Noatak.*

a school and an airfield. A young boy proudly showed us his self-constructed kayak.

We passed on through a fringe of forest toward the coast. Once more hills forced the Noatak into a huge oxbow. Then it stretched south at Mulik Hills, spreading into a large delta at the ocean. Rotting, abandoned fox farms and a few silent, scattered cabins mutely spoke of life and death on the river. A fishing boat ferried us across the choppy sea to Kotzebue, the end of a memorable journey.

(*See map page 149.*)

The Aniak

River of the Bears

Coming down a tributary creek to the main stream of the Aniak, we saw fresh bear tracks. We paddled, lined and drifted down the small creek. The scenery was magnificent—mountains and snowfields, hills and tundra. In the early evening we saw trees, a truly welcome sight. I like to sleep under a tree, and we wanted some dry firewood. It rained all night and the next day, so we stayed around the camp. I rigged an additional shelter with a plastic tarp.

We were doing the laundry, when Brigitte said she heard a bear. I thought she must be imagining things, but she walked over to the tent and was eye-to-eye with a black bear. Pale and almost voiceless, she came back to inform me that there was indeed a bear. My gun wasn't operable, so walking over with my little hand ax and my best manners, I asked the bruin to please leave. The bear retreated a few feet, stood there shaking his head and then decided to comply with my request. A few hours later when a brown bear came walking toward us, we took to a tree, one I had prepared for a quick ascent after the first bear's visit.

We pushed off the next day, passing a moose browsing on the banks. A black bear was so curious

Left—*The upper Aniak.*

that he came to within 10 feet of us. A little later, we saw three black bears grazing on the banks. A few ducks that we disturbed drifted to within a few feet of the bears but were ignored. As evening approached, the rain began again, and we made camp hurriedly. It rained all day, all night and the day after. The river rose 4 feet, and twice I had to move the boats to higher ground.

Bear tracks on the sandbank.

When we took to the river again, it was a changed stream. The clear, swift waters we had known were gone. In their place was a raging torrent, muddy and full of uprooted trees. The water spilled over into low-lying areas. We had to focus all of our attention on the river to avoid drifting trees and an alarming number of sweepers. We never knew exactly which channel to take.

Every sandbank was covered with bear tracks, and through the trees I glimpsed a brown bear. He must have a hard time catching fish in this muddy torrent, I thought. The river branched out. The bigger arm went to the left, but it was almost closed by a big sweeper, a cottonwood tree that had toppled into the water. We chose the much smaller and slower right branch. Rounding the sandbank, I saw the brown bear again, this time in the middle of the 15-foot-wide stream. He was only 30 feet away as I backed away hurriedly to avoid him. I never knew if he noticed me.

Above—*Bears are numerous along the Aniak.*
Right—*The Aniak, high because of very heavy rains.*

I made it back into the main channel and the torrential current promptly swept me under the sweeper. When I saw that despite my frantic efforts I could not avoid colliding with the sloping tree, I flipped my kayak in an effort to avoid hanging up on the branches. As it happened, the boat and I became inseparable; steel cables from the disengaged rudder assembly formed a noose around my neck. Every time the boat jerked, the noose tightened; it threatened

Brigitte frees her kayak from a pile of driftwood.

to suffocate me. I dropped my paddle. The water was ice-cold, and my waterlogged clothing, which included a raincoat, made it hard for me to swim.

Brigitte had been a few hundred feet behind me. Warned by my signal, she hugged the inside left bank to avoid the sweeper. After what seemed like an eternity, I finally managed to use an eddy and get ground under my feet. I pulled the boat out and emptied it, but there was no place to make a fire.

We started out again; fortunately, I had my spare paddle. Besides a paddle, I had lost a waterproof camera in my bout with the sweeper. We shot down the river for another 2 hours, until we found a tent site with a view of the river and plenty of firewood. Once the fire was going and I had warmed up, I put up the tent while Brigitte cooked pancakes.

After dinner, as we were watching the rampaging river, a brown bear came toward our camp. I pointed my useless gun menacingly at him and made some noise. He took the hint, jumped into the river and crossed it—amazing how well they swim. This was the last bear we saw on the trip.

The next day the water seemed to have risen even more, blurring the transition between river and forest, spilling over the banks and into the trees. Channels kept branching out, and it was only by guesswork and luck that we decided on the right ones. Brigitte once was swept onto a pile of driftwood but managed to free the boat. By late afternoon, the river disappeared. Water boiled and rushed through the trees and under huge logjams. Manhandling the kayaks, we repeatedly cut through thickets, and hauled the boats over logjams and barricades.

A penetrating stench was in the air from hundreds of rotting salmon, some half-eaten by the bears. Understandably, we did not feel very comfortable intruding on the bears' feeding grounds. Giant cottonwoods and black spruce shut out most of the sky, creating a weird atmosphere. Anxious to get out of this waterlogged prison, we worked our way downriver until darkness came. A sandbank with

flooded and fast, at least we could paddle along. Thousands of sea gulls were feeding on the dead salmon. In the afternoon the pace of the current slackened, the river broadened and meandered through the forest.

A log cabin was our first sign of civilization and a reminder that we had seen no other humans for 2 weeks. An empty gas barrel on shore said power boats used this

A moose browses on the bank.

lots of driftwood was our campsite for the night. We did not sleep well, despite a blazing fire, knowing that bears were prowling around and that if the river rose another foot it would flood our camp. But no bears showed and the water receded a few inches.

After another half-day of paddling, lifting, carrying and climbing through an unbelievable maze of fallen trees and driftwood, we finally reached a more confined portion of the river. Although it was

stretch and told us there were no more obstacles on our way to the Kuskokwim.

At seven that night we made our last camp on the river beneath huge cottonwoods. Wild currants covered the floor of the forest. It rained again—all day, all night and the next morning. By late afternoon it finally stopped, and the sun occasionally peeped through the clouds. At last we heard an airplane taking off, and later, a motorboat.
(*See map page 117.*)

The Porcupine River
Hudson's Bay Company Fur Route

Not many river systems offer as rich a historical past and as varied and interesting a present as the Porcupine. Its full length is north of the Arctic Circle. The Porcupine is surrounded by the scenic beauty of forests and has many kinds of wildlife along its shores. The one settlement on its course, Old Crow in Canada's Yukon Territory, is without road access. It is situated about halfway between the head-waters of the Porcupine and its juncture with the Yukon River. More than half of the river flows in Canada.

We had flown the 50 miles from Aklavik on the Mackenzie delta to Summit Lake, about a half-mile from a little creek, Little Bell River, a tributary of the Big Bell of the Porcupine system. The Cessna 180 left us to set up camp in a rainstorm. Though only August 7, it snowed during the night and the next day. Although it was still snowing a day later, we put our two single kayaks, folding boats, to-gether. When the snow stopped, we portaged a half-mile across the tundra to the Little Bell River, the real beginning of our voyage.

The mountains around us made it look as though winter had arrived. Icy gusts raced down the river and drove rain across the valley. We were cold and wet when we found a solitary tree. Expecting some pro-tection from it, we stretched our tarp for a siwash camp, crawled into our sleeping bags and instantly fell asleep. Toward morning, I woke up feeling squeezed. It had snowed 6 inches overnight, and the tarp had collapsed on me under the load of snow. For 2 days it rained and snowed, and the temperature plummeted to 17°. As soon as blue sky showed, we were on our way through the snow.

The Bell River proper, with its now-green banks, led us out of the mountains into the tree-fringed tundra. Countless ducks and geese were preparing for their long journey south. A cow moose and her calf wandered along the bank. A few dilapidated log cabins gave witness to the days when LaPierre House was a bustling place located where the portage route of the fur trade from the Mackenzie Valley met the Bell River.

Good weather continued but it was cold, and the snow in the shadow of the north bank did not melt. We watched a wolf bury a partly eaten carcass and saw a grizzly ambling among the rocks, turning each one over looking for tidbits.

We found a dream campsite on wide grassy banks beside the smooth Porcupine River. Howling all through the night, indicated to us that the caribou were on their yearly migration southward and that the wolves were following.

Right—Snow covered the kayaks during a night on the Little Bell River, part of the Porcupine system.

Clouds moved in, and the temperature rose as we paddled toward Old Crow, an old Indian settlement. At the village we did some socializing, visiting some people I had met years before. In the evening sun, we set out to find a quiet campsite some miles down the river when we were hailed out of the darkening shadow of the trees. Bill Smith, a white man married to an extraordinary Indian woman, invited us to stop for coffee. We ended up staying the night.

The next day we camped to watched for caribou on Caribou Bar Creek. Instead, three grizzlies

Clockwise from right—
The Porcupine River.
A pair of caribou race up the river's bank.
A deserted cabin at Burnt Paw testifies to the long-past activity of the gold rush on the Porcupine.

almost walked into the tent. But we did see many caribou too, trotting along the banks and crossing the powerful current. Some magnificent bulls ran along the boulder-strewn bank at breakneck speed.

The site of Rampart House still has standing buildings, some three-story structures that served the Hudson's Bay Company after it

moved from Fort Yukon. Only the wind or an occasional bear pass through the doors now.

All the way down to the Coleen River cliffs and steep, wooded banks pressed in around the Porcupine. There were fewer caribou, but an occasional moose or black bear put in an appearance. Log cabins along the banks attested to the value of the Porcupine flats as a fur-producing region. The people of Fort Yukon still maintain traplines on the flats. The Black River from the south and the Sheenjek River from the north join the Porcupine just before it empties into the Yukon River at Fort Yukon, our destination.

(*See map page 127.*)

The Copper River
Violent Performance at Breakup

The Copper River, with its huge water volume, cuts through the mountains and glaciers of the Chugach Mountains. It is one of the state's most easily accessible rivers. Traces of civilization left by spurts of development during the past 70 years have not lessened the Copper's spectacular attractions. At the turn of the century a narrow-gauge railroad was built along its banks to the now-abandoned Kennecott Mines. Several settlements on the river can be reached by road. Yet for all its development, a trip down the Copper is still a serious voyage into the wilderness country of sheep, buffalo, moose, bear and seal.

In early May, right after breakup, we crossed frozen puddles on the banks of the river to launch our kayaks. The banks still had remnant shoulders of ice, and the grass had not started to green. Indians at Copper Center warned us that the river might not be open all the way. Because the water was low, we encountered riffles and easy rapids in quick succession. The postmistress in the largely abandoned town of Chitina told us that

Right—The Copper River provides a true wilderness experience, even though it is accessible by road in several places.

our trip was foolish, emphasizing that many people had lost their lives on the river.

We continued our voyage through a valley with wide sweeping views of the Wrangell Mountains. At Wood Canyon, sometimes the scene of whirlpools and huge waves, the mountains crowded in, but we passed without incident. The weather was perfect, but late afternoon winds created dust storms and thrusts on the paddle powerful enough to make very unpleasant paddling conditions. Below the Copper's confluence with the Bremner River, the dusty sand flats ended, and Allen Glacier put its icy snout down to the river. Impressive, snow-clad mountains dominated the river in this part of the valley and there was scant forest growth. Baird Canyon narrowed the 5-mile-wide valley to 100 yards. We faced easy rapids at the entrance to Miles Lake, one of the most spectacular scenic attractions on any river.

Miles Glacier with a broad 3-mile front extends far into the lake. Bob Goodwin, an Alaskan sourdough and mountain climber, told me that he and a friend almost had lost their lives at Miles Glacier, when they had run the river several years earlier. As they coasted below ice overhangs where the Copper had cut its course through the glacier, their boat capsized, and they were dumped out on an ice shelf. At our passing, however, the river was low, and the lake was calm—too calm, it was frozen solid.

It was only 3 miles to the outlet, but low water had exposed miles of soft, quicksandy mud. We often got stuck and had to use our mud-bound boats to lift our bodies and our rubber boots out of the mud. We spent most of the day getting across the mud flats to open water. The water was open but not navigable. Low water had created rapids over exposed boulders, and the river was clogged with ice. We managed to force our way downstream, finally retiring to a high sandbank for safety and camp.

From this vantage point we had a front row seat to a violent performance by nature. Wherever masses of ice dammed the river, the increasing water pressure caused chunks of ice weighing several tons to shoot 20 feet into the air. Cracks in the ice, hundreds of yards long, opened up, grinding football field-sized ice cakes to slush. We were awed prisoners for 2 days before we

The Copper River in early May.

A moment of peace on the Copper River just after breakup.

dared seek a safe route out of the ocean of jumbled ice. Once we got to open water we decided to paddle around the coast and up the Eyak River to Cordova.

June was nesting time, and thousands of ducks, geese, swans and Arctic terns flocked to the marsh around us. We had ample time to watch them for the slough we had picked to travel to the Gulf of Alaska on the Pacific Ocean turned out to be more of a wet road than a stream. The 1964 earthquake had lifted the whole area 8 feet leaving the flats high and dry except at high tide.

We finally managed to drag our boats out to the ocean shore but were not fast enough to follow the retreating low tide. We were stuck in the mud for the next 10 hours, sitting in the boats waiting for the water to return. With the next high tide, we were able to get to the gulf and on to the Eyak River and Cordova.

(*See map page 91.*)

The Chilikadrotna
Fast River Through the Forest

West of Anchorage across the Alaska and Aleutian ranges, a score of short, fast rivers flow west through the forest. Most of these streams are born in lakes, remnants of the last ice age. Some of the most picturesque, a pair called Twin Lakes, is the origin of the Chilikadrotna River. In late June our chartered bush plane banked for a landing on one of the Twin Lakes, the beginning of an expedition for Brigitte and me.

When our aircraft had departed, we took our time assembling the two single, folding kayaks and leisurely set up camp. The sun was hot and we enjoyed walking barefoot on the fine, warm sand. Once under way, 15 miles of paddling brought us to the west end of the lake. There we heard the sound of the first rapids. Scouting

the riffles, I saw some large grayling and decided that we would camp near the rapids. We found a perfect site halfway through the whitewater, and in 20 minutes a couple of nice grayling sizzled in the pan.

Next morning, we continued through the rapids for a half-mile and then ran 3 miles of fast water that swept us along through a forest. For several miles from there on, the current slackened visibly, the river widened and the trees gave way to grassy tundra. Reentering the forest, the pace of the river quickened appreciably with fast water and rapids. By midafternoon the sun was shining up the stream and into our faces making it impossible for us to spot shallows and boulders in time to outmaneuver them. It was a good excuse to stop early and make camp at a perfect spot with scattered trees, mossy ground and a little stream.

The rest was needed, for the next day was our white-water day, not really difficult, but taxing enough to require alertness at all times. On one stretch, the river dropped 50

Sepp on the upper Chilikadrotna.

The Chilikadrotna flows through the forested hills of Western Alaska.

feet in three-quarters of a mile. Trees whipped by as we negotiated rapid after rapid. Our heavily laden boats responded sluggishly and required all of our strength. Tired, we stopped at the Little Mulchatna River to camp.

The gradient gradually decreased the next day, but the current was still swift. A few logjams forced us to get out of the boats, and sweepers kept us alert. A high bank offered a welcome campsite on the river, and some terrific rainbow fishing. With a fire burning, we watched the evening progress. An otter hurried across the gravel bar carrying a fish in its mouth. Later that night, a cow moose browsing opposite our campsite splashed loudly through the river.

When we resumed our journey, the river valley turned marshy and small islands appeared. As the channels narrowed, the sky was blocked out by the dense green forest, and the river gained speed. Most often, however, it flowed quietly past huge beaver lodges toward its end at the Mulchatna River.

(See map page 119.)

VOYAGING
THE WILD RIVERS

This book is not a guide for novices. Even for those experienced in river travel, this book is designed only to stimulate inquiry, not to offer final answers. It is not intended as an absolute step-by-step guide to any of the wild rivers. The rivers are alive—in a state of flux. There are few constants.

Before starting a voyage, maps must be gathered and interpreted. Predeparture activities must include physical conditioning, equipment checks, purchase of supplies, a consideration of emergency procedures and some thought of transportation needs and communication possibilities. All of these elements must be incorporated into planning a voyage North.

Choosing a Craft

The first thing to consider before making a voyage on a wild river is what type of craft to use. The oldest controllable craft is the raft. It has taken many forms and shapes: several logs tied together; inflated animal skins; a gang of gas cans or barrels; and in recent years, commercial rubber rafts. The most popular rafts today are those made of tough rubber materials, inflatable in several sections and large enough to float over obstacles while retaining maneuverability. Larger rafts use sweepers; small ones are controlled by oars.

Canoes and kayaks are the craft best suited to wilderness travel. There is no better way to identify with old-time voyagers than to paddle small boats

Overleaf—*Voyaging the Aniuk River.*
Below—*Fiberglass kayaks and collapsible, folding boats.*

Decked, fiberglass canoes.

along the same waterways they traveled. The canoe has returned to its rightful place on the wilderness waterways of America. The kayak, the "newcomer" from the Arctic Ocean, is earning a growing number of enthusiasts. Each kind of craft has its supporters, and each offers some special advantage under certain conditions. Choice frequently hinges on a given paddler's experience. The choice of a craft should be based on the skill of the user and the boat's suitability for the voyage.

A modern, lightweight canoe of aluminum or fiberglass will take the traveler anywhere. With a splash cover or deck, it is suitable for white water. It can carry two people and a great amount of gear in relative comfort and safety. For most uses it is preferable to the smaller two-man kayaks that force people to sit too close together and have limited storage space. The single blade that propels canoes, however, takes more skill to use effectively than the kayak's double paddle. The high freeboard of a canoe is a disadvantage when there is a high wind.

The kayak, originally used for hunting in coastal waters, was designed for surf or rolling waves. Modern adaptations have made it quite suitable for wilderness travel, and it is a good performer in difficult white water. Most modern kayaks are made of fiberglass. A version extremely popular in Alaska is a collapsible, folding boat that can be disassembled and packed in bags for easy transport. These kayaks are available as singles or as doubles. Most models have air flotation devices built in to make them unsinkable.

Clockwise from top—
Equipment should be checked periodically.
Repairing a damaged kayak.
A stop for repairs on a collapsible kayak pierced by a stick.
Opposite page—Small plane is the only means of access to many of Alaska's wild rivers.

Preparation and Equipment

Many things must be considered for a project to take shape. Obviously, the amount of time available will determine how long the voyage can last. June is the flood month, a time to stay away from the large rivers, but a good month to run small rivers after snow melt and runoff.

If portages are contemplated, the weight of gear and food should be kept to a minimum without skimping on essentials. These essentials include: a short, thin sleeping mat, a lightweight down or Fiberfill II-type sleeping bag, a light waterproof tent, cookware, food staples, at least one full set of extra clothes, a repair kit and spare parts for the boat, and a medical kit. Optional equipment that is less necessary, but desirable, includes: fishing gear, a helmet, a supply of repellent to combat the ever-present mosquitoes, emergency signals, smoke flares, signal dyes and a signal mirror.

Transportation

Transportation is a problem of special significance in Alaska because of the state's vast area and the scarcity of roads. Any water voyage away from the road frequently involves a long walk or expensive air transportation. Folding kayaks or rubber rafts can reduce the expense because passengers and gear can move in one trip. Although some air taxi operators will tie rigid kayaks or canoes to their floats, regulations do not allow passengers to be transported at the same time.

Most settlements in Alaska are served by regularly scheduled mail planes, usually the least expensive way to ship camping gear, folding boats, food and the traveler. On the Yukon, Tanana, Porcupine, Koyukuk and Kuskokwim rivers another alternative is sometimes possible, transportation by barge.

Challenge and Ability

The ability to challenge increasingly difficult tasks grows as skills are developed. Paddling is no exception. Many of Alaska's rivers are not technically difficult to paddle, but it is always safest to have a margin of skill beyond the degree of challenge. A canoeist's or a kayaker's skill helps increase the level of enjoyment found on any voyage.

Prospective voyagers may use this generally acceptable scale of paddler's skills as an aid in determining whether or not they have the level of skill necessary to run a particular wild river. The classifications specify the skills with which a paddler should be completely comfortable before attempting a river with the same numerical designation (see page 58). Thus, a voyager should be well skilled in the techniques listed for a Class II paddler before running a WW2 (Grade 2) river.

Class   I—A beginner, knows basic strokes and can handle a boat in smooth water.

Class II—A novice, can effectively manage basic white-water strokes in a kayak or in both the bow or stern of a canoe, can read water.

Class III—Can negotiate rapids requiring complex maneuvers, can use eddy turns and basic bow-upstream techniques, skillful in intermediate rapids.

Class IV—Expert, can run difficult rapids in canoe or kayak, can handle heavy water and complex rapids.

Class V—Senior leader, has expert skills plus wide experience and good judgment necessary to lead trips on any river.

Constant training builds good habits and quick reflexes. Any hour spent in a boat will add something to an individual's store of experience and knowledge. Canoe clubs, kayak schools, white-water manuals and experienced friends are sources of information on technical matters. But the most refined technique cannot completely offset poor physical conditioning or a lack of stamina.

Left—It is always safest to have a margin of skill beyond what the river demands.
Below—Difficult rapids require a high degree of skill.

Clockwise from upper left—
Kayakers paddle through reeds on the Aniuk River.
*Portaging a collapsible kayak between the Redstone
and Cutler rivers.*
*Adverse conditions sometimes demand dragging the
boat around sweepers.*
Boats must be lined in shallow water.
Riffles are encountered on many wild rivers.

Stopping for rest when needed is an important guideline to safety.

Judging Objectively

To travel over long distances for extended periods of time without crises or hair-raising emergencies is, of course, the goal of any sensible paddler. This translates into an ability to recognize a potential problem or danger, before it becomes an emergency. The talent to make critical judgments can be developed best with the help of experienced guidance in controlled situations. The limits of both physical endurance and technical ability will grow together with practice.

Underestimating ability can be troublesome; overestimating can be fatal. Stopping for rest when it's needed, and quitting for the day before exhaustion are important guidelines that contribute to safety and enjoyment. Alaska's long summer days are an advantage. After a day's paddle, a few hours relaxing in the soft evening sun or going on a casual hike can help travelers gear down.

What's an average day? In my experience, 50 miles a day on large rivers that have 5-mph currents is a very good distance. Twenty-five miles may be all that can be paddled on a slow meandering river. Eight hours of paddling represents a hard day's work.

Evaluating The Rivers

Any river is difficult, or dangerous, in proportion to the complexity of the course, the volume of water and the rate of descent, the gradient. Paddlers must remember that any river's ratings depend not only on the topographical characteristics, but also on fluctuations in water volume.

Getting a long-distance view of a stretch of water.

Any unfamiliar stretch of water that is not clearly readable from the boat should be reconnoitered first on foot.

Judging a river begins at home. Imagination paints a picture of a given river on the basis of available information. But once on a river, look first for clues to water volume. In general, low water means a technically more demanding but safer path. There is less water to maneuver, but also less water for tricky eddies or powerful wave action. The current is slower.

Higher water foretells faster currents, more powerful wave and eddy actions, easier upsets and usually colder water. Especially dangerous by-products of high water are uprooted trees and sweepers. They should be avoided by taking evasive action well above the obstruction, because flow diversion and deceleration cause obstacles of this type to exert attracting forces on boats.

The gradient, or rate of drop, usually is measured in feet per mile. Gradient can be estimated by studying the contour intervals on the topographic maps available from the U.S. Geological Survey. Most white-water rivers have a descent of between 20 and 60 feet per mile. A gradient of less than 20 feet per mile usually indicates a river with moving water but no difficult rapids, WWI (Grade 1). A gradient of more than 50 feet per mile normally suggests a more difficult river, WW4 (Grade 4).

In general, the easiest and safest channels are those with the highest flow and velocity. They are the deepest, least obstructed part of a riverbed. Silty waters, however, make it difficult to recognize water level over gravel bars and other obstacles. After rain, rivers can rise substantially to cause many unforeseen difficulties and dangerous conditions. In those situations, a layover is advisable. Better 3 days late than 30 years too early.

The volume of water determines the actual difficulty of the river.

Over the years, a set of guidelines has been developed to standardize ratings of the difficulties posed by specific rivers, or sections of them. The ratings can help river travelers decide whether or not their skills are up to the challenge. Because relatively few Alaskan rivers have been rated formally, those planning a voyage must often make estimates from maps.

The charts in this book follow the standard grading system, Grades 1 to 6, to aid in the selection of a suitable watercourse. Additionally, a system of flat-water ratings is used for rivers that do not present white-water difficulties under average circumstances. The standard grades are expressed as white-water ratings or WW1 to WW6. Flat-water ratings are denoted as FW1 to FW3.

Ratings apply to the technical difficulties present at average waterflow. In all cases, the volume of water flowing through the river at the time of passage determines the actual difficulty of the river. An increased water volume can turn a river that normally is WW2 (Grade 2) into a much more difficult river, a WW4 (Grade 4). A less than normal water volume can increase the difficulty of a stream by exposing rocks that had posed no problem. Ratings are for *normal* conditions only.

For the purposes of this guidebook, I have expanded the standard rating system to include an indication of the type of craft suggested for each classification of water. A boat is indicated for use on a particular river only if it can be used on the whole course of the river. I have not classified rubber rafts or riverboats in the main grading system, but I have indicated their suitability on the river charts.

All ratings given for rivers in this volume are approximate. Relatively few Alaskan rivers have been rated formally. Frequently voyagers must make their own estimates as part of their pre-trip planning. Maps can be ordered from the U. S. Geological Survey, Map Sales Office, 508 W. Second Avenue, Anchorage, Alaska 99501.

White-Water Classifications

The ratings WW1-WW6 are equivalent to the standard Grades 1-6. See page 51 for the paddler's skills requisite for each water classification.

WW1
C1 + C2—K1 + K2—Oc
Very easy—small regular waves, sandbanks, riffles.

WW2
C1 + C2—K1 + K2—Oc
Easy—rapids of medium difficulty, wide, clear passages, low benches.

WW3
C1 + C2—K1 + K2
Medium—numerous high irregular waves, rapids with narrow passages require expertise in maneuver, inspection needed, splash cover mandatory.

WW4
C1 + C2—K1
Difficult—rocks and dangerous eddies, passages difficult to reconnoiter, inspection mandatory the first time, powerful and exact maneuvering necessary, Eskimo roll desirable, crash helmet and boat flotation mandatory.

WW5
C2 + K1
Very difficult—long, very violent and extremely difficult rapids, no letup in riverbed obstructions, violent current, big ledges, very steep gradient, reconnoitering essential but difficult, Eskimo roll mandatory.

WW6
C2 + K1
Extraordinarily difficult—Grade 5 carried to extremes of navigability, almost impossible and very dangerous, only for teams of experts with rescue team on bank.

Flat water on a good day, the Nigu River.

Flat-Water Classifications

These ratings, developed specifically for this book, designate streams that do not present white-water difficulties under normal conditions.

FW1   Standing water or slow-flowing water.
FW2   Current that can be overcome by backpaddling.
FW3   Current faster than backpaddling, some skill needed for bends and back eddies.

Craft Classifications

(Oc)   Open canoe
(C1)   Decked one-man canoe
(C2)   Decked two-man canoe
(K1)   Decked one-man kayak*

(K2)   Decked two-man kayak
(R)   Raft, primarily rubber raft
(Rb)   Riverboat, motor powered

*Above Grade 4 in this rating, K1 means fiberglass kayak. Below Grade 4, K1 may mean a quality folding kayak.

River Access

AA   Access by air
AB   Access by boat

AR   Access by road

U. S. Coast Guard regulations require an approved life jacket for each passenger in each boat. Every paddler must wear a life jacket and a wet suit when traveling rivers rated above WW2 (Grade 2). WW3 (Grade 3) requires craft to be equipped with splash covers.

Fifty-three Rivers

These sketches provide basic information on a select group of waterways for prospective paddlers of Alaska's wild rivers. The choice of rivers represented here is small, but this list is representative of many, many more waiting to be explored. Many rivers are remote, and there is a scarcity of factual, verified information available on them for all seasons and all conditions.

These recommendations are based on average conditions and average water volumes. The difficulty of a given river can change drastically. Certainly at some time someone has used, or will use, a craft not included

Headwaters of the Nigu River.

in one of my river descriptions. I feel, however, that my recommendations can lead to sensible, safe voyages, assuming average water conditions.

These sketches give only basic suggestions about a specific river. All ratings and distances specified here are approximate. Prospective voyagers should seek as much additional information as possible. Order maps from the U.S. Geological Survey, Map Sales Office, 508 W. Second Avenue, Anchorage, Alaska 99501. Information on charter planes is available from the Alaska Division of Tourism, Pouch E, Juneau, Alaska 99811. Personal involvement in planning is essential to a satisfying trip.

1

Fortymile River

In late summer the Fortymile may be low, making a safer but slower voyage.

This is an excellent waterway that has a historic significance dating back to the gold mining era. Depending on the water volume, it is a moderately fast river with series of rapids spaced several miles apart. The rapids become progressively more difficult downstream. All rapids can be checked out on foot first or easily portaged if the need arises. In late July and August the river may be very low, making a safer but slower voyage. Access is by road at three points in Alaska, as well as at Clinton, Yukon Territory, Canada. Travelers must report to Canadian customs before entering Canada. The float can be continued down the Yukon River over one of its most scenic stretches to terminate at either Eagle or Circle, Alaska. Road access exists to both towns.

River Location

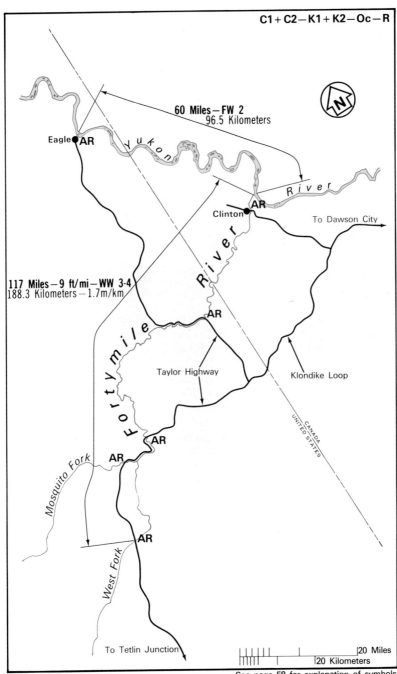

C1 + C2 − K1 + K2 − Oc − R

N

60 Miles — FW 2
96.5 Kilometers

Eagle ● AR

Yukon

River

Clinton ● AR

To Dawson City

117 Miles — 9 ft/mi — WW 3-4
188.3 Kilometers — 1.7m/km

Fortymile River

AR

Taylor Highway

Klondike Loop

CANADA
UNITED STATES

AR

Mosquito Fork   AR   AR

West Fork

AR

To Tetlin Junction

20 Miles
20 Kilometers

See page 58 for explanation of symbols.

2

Lyon Creek, Granite Creek, Sixmile Creek, East Fork Sixmile Creek

These creeks form a superb white-water combination in the heart of the Kenai Peninsula. It is easily accessible with fast water for all levels of ability. At the proper water level, this creek system can be run from Lyon Creek in the valley just below Turnagain Pass, to sea level, a drop of about 900 feet. At low water level put in at Bertha Creek campground. It is fast but not dangerous water, although logs commonly found across the creek at several places demand quick reaction.

East Fork Sixmile Creek is a cold, clear, swift mountain stream in a beautiful setting. Sweepers and logs can be hazards. The difficult part of this white-water trip begins approximately 3 miles above the Hope Access Road where the river is narrowed by granite cliffs into a canyon. **Only experienced paddlers should continue beyond this point.** Steep chutes, narrowed by boulders, alternate with placid pools. After leaving the canyon the course is extremely difficult with hazardous rapids and falls. There is almost no letup to mark the lower section of the river until about 2 miles before it enters Turnagain Arm.

River Location

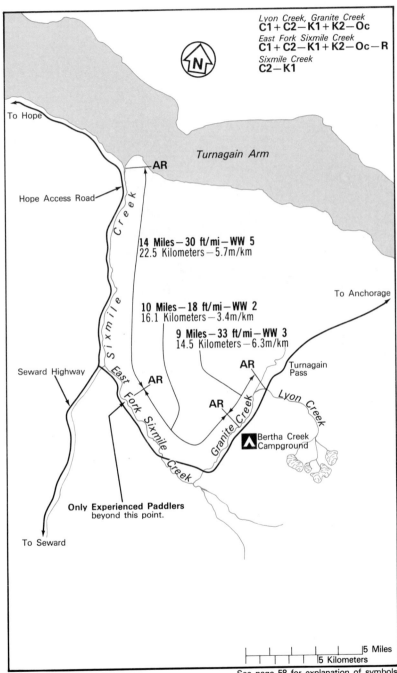

Lyon Creek, Granite Creek
C1 + C2 — K1 + K2 — Oc
East Fork Sixmile Creek
C1 + C2 — K1 + K2 — Oc — R
Sixmile Creek
C2 — K1

To Hope

Turnagain Arm

AR

Hope Access Road

Creek

14 Miles — 30 ft/mi — WW 5
22.5 Kilometers — 5.7m/km

Sixmile

10 Miles — 18 ft/mi — WW 2
16.1 Kilometers — 3.4m/km

To Anchorage

9 Miles — 33 ft/mi — WW 3
14.5 Kilometers — 6.3m/km

Seward Highway

East Fork Sixmile Creek

AR

AR

AR

Turnagain
Pass

Granite Creek

Lyon Creek

▲ Bertha Creek
Campground

Only Experienced Paddlers
beyond this point.

To Seward

|5 Miles
|5 Kilometers

See page 58 for explanation of symbols.

3

Nenana River

The braided channels of the Nenana do not have the difficult rapids found in its upper reaches.

Easily accessible, the middle course of the Nenana River is one of the most popular, as well as one of the most difficult, white-water rivers in Alaska. The Denali Highway permits access to the river where it is beautifully clear and fast. However, sweepers and sharp bends are numerous. Flowing beside the George Parks Highway, the Nenana has only occasional rapids until it passes Mt. McKinley Village Resort. **From this point to below Healy, heavy water and very difficult rapids make the river suitable only for expert paddlers.** Others should skirt this section by leapfrogging it on the George Parks Highway. Below this canyon area, the Nenana's course to its mouth on the Tanana River has braided channels, but contains no difficult rapids. Moose and bear are seen often on this lower stretch of the river, with the Alaska Range and Mount McKinley, a backdrop looming in the south.

River Location

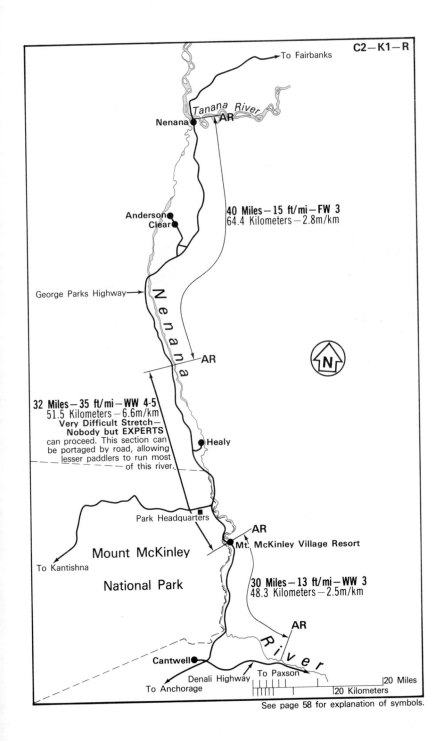

C2—K1—R

→ To Fairbanks

Tanana River

Nenana ● ⊢AR

40 Miles — 15 ft/mi — FW 3
64.4 Kilometers — 2.8m/km

Anderson ●
Clear ●

George Parks Highway →

N e n a n a

⊢AR

32 Miles — 35 ft/mi — WW 4-5
51.5 Kilometers — 6.6m/km
**Very Difficult Stretch —
Nobody but EXPERTS**
can proceed. This section can
be portaged by road, allowing
lesser paddlers to run most
of this river.

● Healy

Park Headquarters ■

⊢AR

Mount McKinley

To Kantishna

National Park

Mt ● McKinley Village Resort

30 Miles — 13 ft/mi — WW 3
48.3 Kilometers — 2.5m/km

R i v e r

AR

Cantwell ●

Denali Highway   To Paxson

To Anchorage

⎮20 Miles

⎮20 Kilometers

See page 58 for explanation of symbols.

Delta River

The Delta River spills from the rugged Alaska Range to form a braided course in its lower reaches.

Braided, silty and ice-cold, the Delta is a challenging white-water river for the expert. Access is by the Denali Highway at Tangle Lakes; falls below the lakes necessitate a quarter-mile portage on the right bank. For the first 3 miles there are difficult rapids. A half-dozen wrecked and abandoned canoes along this stretch testify to the degree of challenge. Below the rapids, it is easy traveling and good grayling fishing. All paddlers take out at the Richardson Highway and drive north around the Black Rapids before putting in again. This stretch of the Delta is difficult, very fast and braided for approximately 30 miles before it widens into a broad valley. Channels constantly intertwine and separate before they merge into the Tanana River. Access by road is possible at several places along the river. **Caution: Only well-qualified experts should attempt to run the Black Rapids.**

River Location

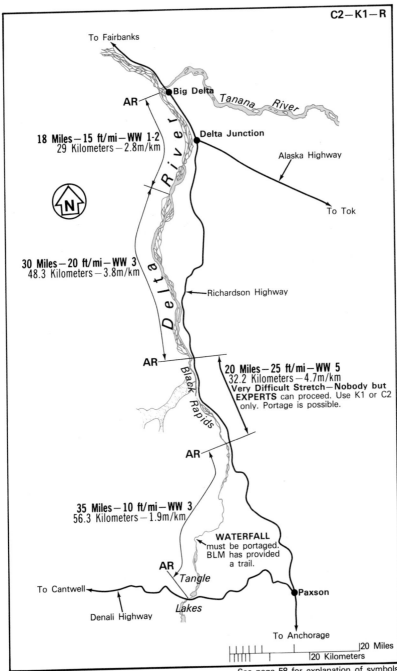

C2—K1—R

To Fairbanks

Big Delta

AR

Tanana River

Delta River

18 Miles—15 ft/mi—WW 1-2
29 Kilometers—2.8m/km

Delta Junction

Alaska Highway

To Tok

N

30 Miles—20 ft/mi—WW 3
48.3 Kilometers—3.8m/km

Richardson Highway

AR

Black Rapids

20 Miles—25 ft/mi—WW 5
32.2 Kilometers—4.7m/km
**Very Difficult Stretch—Nobody but
EXPERTS** can proceed. Use K1 or C2
only. Portage is possible.

AR

35 Miles—10 ft/mi—WW 3
56.3 Kilometers—1.9m/km

WATERFALL
must be portaged.
BLM has provided
a trail.

AR

Tangle

To Cantwell

Paxson

Denali Highway

Lakes

To Anchorage

20 Miles

20 Kilometers

See page 58 for explanation of symbols.

5

Susitna River
(Upper)

A few miles from its origin the Susitna, a large glacial river, emerges from the eastern Alaska Range. The mountains provide a magnificent backdrop to the swift, silty water. The best access by road is at the Susitna River Bridge. Braided gravel flats alternate with a single river course; some difficult rapids are in this section. Sparse forest growth clings to the shores along the river. Approximately 30 miles downriver from the bridge, the beautiful Maclaren River joins from the east. After 10 miles of braided gravelly flats, the Tyone River comes in from the east.

The Tyone connects Lake Louise and the Susitna. The slow, meandering Tyone can be used as a connecting waterway to leave the Susitna Valley for the extensive Lake Louise plains. A small outboard motor on a canoe speeds an otherwise slow upriver paddle. It takes about a day to get to Tyone Lake in a canoe with a small motor.

Below its juncture with the Tyone, the Susitna has several huge oxbow bends and approximately 20 miles of swift water and rapids. A tamer section of river is followed by the treacherous Devil Canyon, a section that cannot be paddled. Look for Log Creek on the left, shortly after a sharp right bend (sometimes a riverboat is anchored there). From this point it is possible to portage to Stephan Lake where there is a lodge or to fly out to Talkeetna or Anchorage. **This trip is for experienced wilderness travelers only.** Animals along the river include moose, bear, caribou, wolf and beaver.

River Location

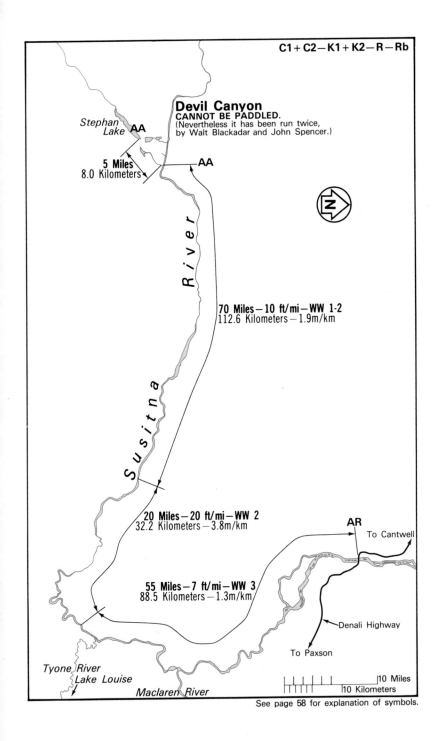

C1 + C2 — K1 + K2 — R — Rb

Devil Canyon
CANNOT BE PADDLED.
(Nevertheless it has been run twice,
by Walt Blackadar and John Spencer.)

Stephan Lake **AA**

AA

5 Miles
8.0 Kilometers

River

Susitna

70 Miles — 10 ft/mi — WW 1-2
112.6 Kilometers — 1.9m/km

20 Miles — 20 ft/mi — WW 2
32.2 Kilometers — 3.8m/km

AR

To Cantwell

55 Miles — 7 ft/mi — WW 3
88.5 Kilometers — 1.3m/km

Denali Highway

To Paxson

Tyone River
Lake Louise

Maclaren River

10 Miles
10 Kilometers

See page 58 for explanation of symbols.

⑥ Maclaren River

A beautiful river in the Alaska Range near Mount Hayes, the Maclaren flows from the high tundra country into the forests of the Lake Louise basin. It can be reached from the Denali Highway. The river is swift and rocky with many shallow rapids. Voyagers should take plenty of materials for boat repair. Water volume can change rapidly. Wildlife along the way includes bear, moose and caribou. Once on the Susitna River, it is possible to exit via the Tyone River to the road at Lake Louise. It is also possible to continue down the Susitna River to the portage to Stephan Lake.

River Location

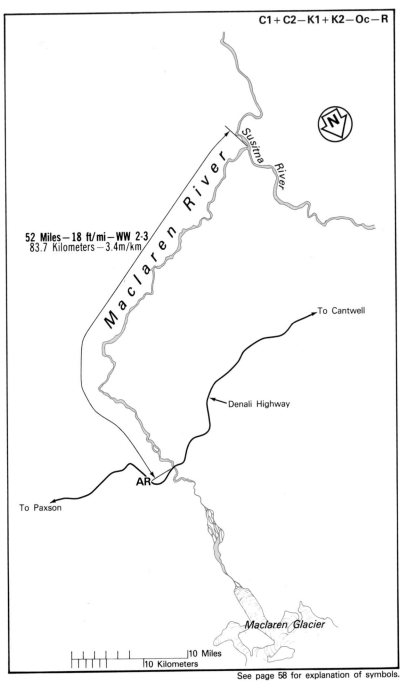

C1+C2−K1+K2−Oc−R

Maclaren River

Susitna River

52 Miles − 18 ft/mi − WW 2-3
83.7 Kilometers − 3.4m/km

To Cantwell

Denali Highway

AR

To Paxson

Maclaren Glacier

10 Miles
10 Kilometers

See page 58 for explanation of symbols.

(7) Tyone River

This route is suitable for riverboats and canoes with small motors as well as for kayaks and paddled canoes. Half the distance is across three adjoining lakes—Louise, Susitna and Tyone. The river flows slowly and meanders, so it can be run upstream by strong paddlers. A wilderness tour in itself, the route also serves as access to the Susitna River. This is a good trip for less experienced paddlers who are experienced outdoor travelers.

River Location

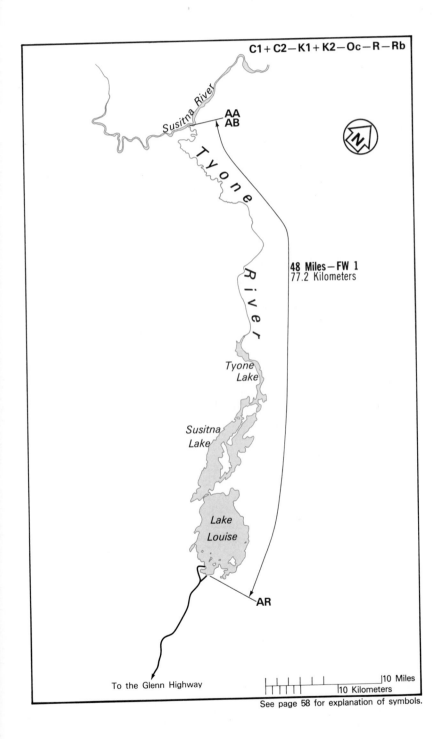

C1 + C2 — K1 + K2 — Oc — R — Rb

Susitna River

AA
AB

T y o n e

R i v e r

48 Miles — FW 1
77.2 Kilometers

Tyone Lake

Susitna Lake

Lake Louise

AR

To the Glenn Highway

|10 Miles
|10 Kilometers

See page 58 for explanation of symbols.

8

Chulitna River, Tokositna River

The Chulitna is a glacier river of consequence. The Middle Fork is accessible at a bridge on the George Parks Highway just below Broad Pass. The East Fork can be reached from the same highway farther south. From the railroad station at Colorado an old mining road leads to the river. Exit from the river is possible at a bridge near the southern boundary of the Denali State Park or at Talkeetna. The upper sections of the river offer exciting white water. Fallen trees and sweepers are a special danger. The water volume can change the river drastically. From the bridge near Denali State Park to Talkeetna, it's an easy river to float, although it's still fast and very cold. **Only skilled white-water paddlers with wilderness river experience should test the section north of the Chulitna Bridge.**

One of the most spectacular scenic, yet easy to run rivers is the Tokositna. It has glaciers along its course and towering Mount McKinley above it. The Tokositna River can be reached in a few minutes by air from Talkeetna. Its flow is moderately swift, but it presents no special obstacles down to its confluence with the Chulitna River just above a bridge on the George Parks Highway. The possibility of continuing south to Talkeetna and on down the lower Susitna River can make this the first leg of a real wilderness voyage with several points accessible by road.

River Location

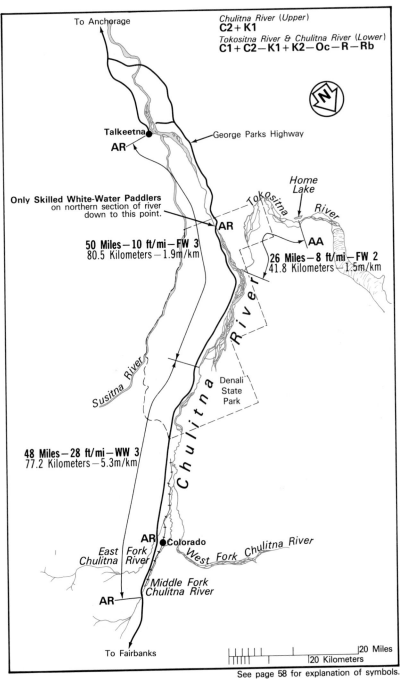

To Anchorage

Chulitna River (Upper)
C2 + K1
Tokositna River & Chulitna River (Lower)
C1 + C2 — K1 + K2 — Oc — R — Rb

Talkeetna
AR

George Parks Highway

Home Lake

Tokositna River

Only Skilled White-Water Paddlers on northern section of river down to this point.

AR

50 Miles — 10 ft/mi — FW 3
80.5 Kilometers — 1.9m/km

AA

26 Miles — 8 ft/mi — FW 2
41.8 Kilometers — 1.5m/km

Chulitna River

Susitna River

Denali State Park

48 Miles — 28 ft/mi — WW 3
77.2 Kilometers — 5.3m/km

AR ●Colorado

East Fork Chulitna River

West Fork Chulitna River

Middle Fork Chulitna River

AR

To Fairbanks

20 Miles
20 Kilometers

See page 58 for explanation of symbols.

(9) Kahiltna River

The Kahiltna is accessible by air just a few miles from where it emerges from the 50-mile-long Kahiltna Glacier. The braided river flows through an immense valley. Above the confluence with Peters Creek, the pace quickens appreciably with huge boulders creating numerous rapids. Silty and ice-cold, it is a challenging river with many optional routes for the skillful paddler. Voyagers may exit by air at the Yentna River or may continue the journey down the Yentna to the Susitna River and Cook Inlet.

River Location

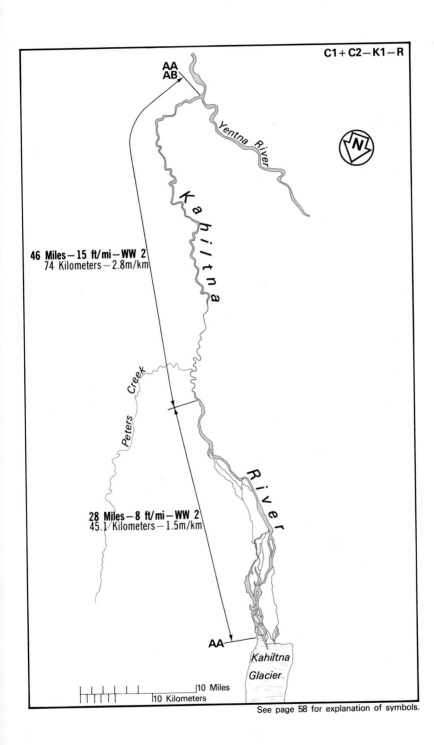

See page 58 for explanation of symbols.

⑩ Yentna River

From its glacial origin this tributary of the Susitna River winds in graceful sweeps through the basin south of Mount McKinley. It is a river with a large water volume. White-water problems are minimal, but sweepers, logjams and floating trees demand caution and skillful boat handling. Moose and bear may be encountered, and good fishing is found on any of the clear-water streams and creeks. Riverboats ply its waters. Several homesteads are located along its forested banks.

River Location

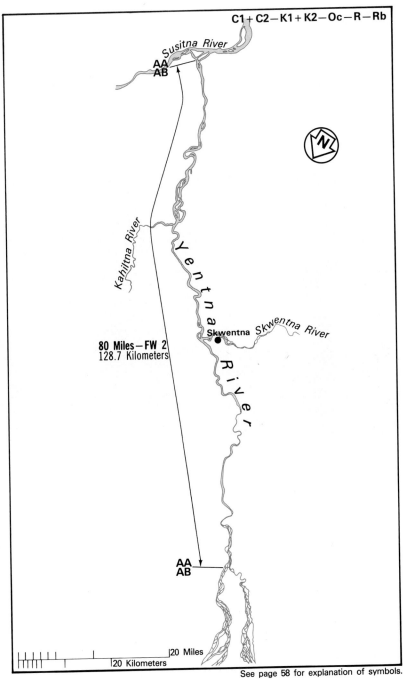

C1 + C2 — K1 + K2 — Oc — R — Rb

Susitna River

AA
AB

Kahiltna River

Yentna River

Skwentna Skwentna River

80 Miles — FW 2
128.7 Kilometers

AA
AB

20 Miles

20 Kilometers

See page 58 for explanation of symbols.

(11) Susitna River
(Lower)

The multichanneled course of the lower Susitna tests the paddler's water-judging abilities.

Mount McKinley dominates this large river. It poses no great technical difficulties, although the multichanneled silty river does test water-judging abilities. Accessible points are the railroad station at Gold Creek and several highway and road approaches north of Willow. Some branches and sloughs may be blocked by logjams and may pose a real danger, even to riverboats which also frequent this river.

River Location

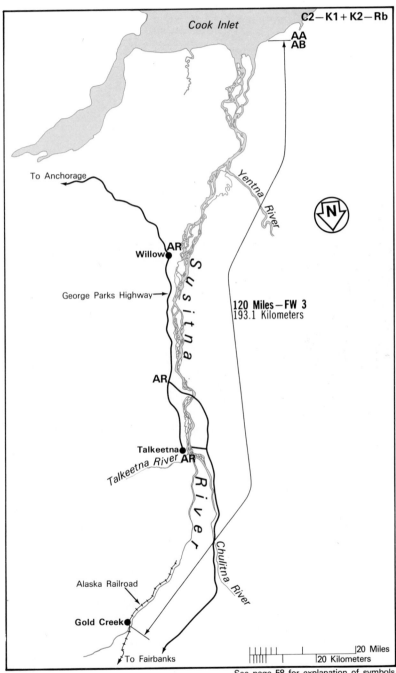

Cook Inlet

C2 — K1 + K2 — Rb

AA
AB

To Anchorage

Yentna River

AR
Willow

George Parks Highway

Susitna River

120 Miles — FW 3
193.1 Kilometers

AR

Talkeetna AR

Talkeetna River

River

Chulitna River

Alaska Railroad

Gold Creek

20 Miles
20 Kilometers

To Fairbanks

See page 58 for explanation of symbols.

12

Skwentna River

One of the most difficult and remote, but spectacular wild rivers in Alaska, is the Skwentna. The difficult portage to its headwaters by way of Chakachamna Lake takes at least a week. Its headwaters under Mount Spurr also can be reached by helicopter. The Skwentna is extremely fast. Its many very difficult rapids and inaccessible canyons make it a wilderness voyage second to none. **This voyage is only for expert paddlers and experienced wilderness travelers above the confluence with the Yentna.** The village of Skwentna, a settlement near the Yentna, has scheduled mail plane service to Anchorage.

Continuing on to the Yentna and the Susitna River down to Cook Inlet can make this trip a major voyage. Some paddlers have paddled from the mouth of the Susitna River into Anchorage along the coast of Cook Inlet, a very treacherous stretch of open water. Moose, bear and an occasional wolf may be encountered.

River Location

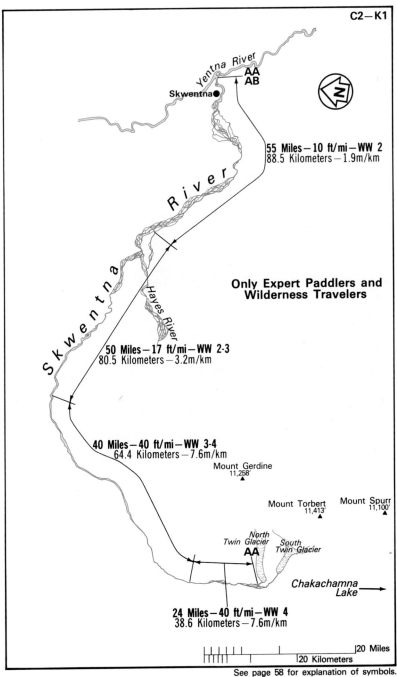

C2—K1

Yentna River

AA
AB

Skwentna●

55 Miles—10 ft/mi—WW 2
88.5 Kilometers—1.9m/km

River

Skwentna

Hayes River

**Only Expert Paddlers and
Wilderness Travelers**

50 Miles—17 ft/mi—WW 2-3
80.5 Kilometers—3.2m/km

40 Miles—40 ft/mi—WW 3-4
64.4 Kilometers—7.6m/km

Mount Gerdine
11,258'
▲

Mount Torbert
11,413'
▲

Mount Spurr
11,100'
▲

North
Twin Glacier
Twin Glacier
AA
South
Twin Glacier

Chakachamna
Lake →

24 Miles—40 ft/mi—WW 4
38.6 Kilometers—7.6m/km

20 Miles

20 Kilometers

See page 58 for explanation of symbols.

13

Little Susitna River

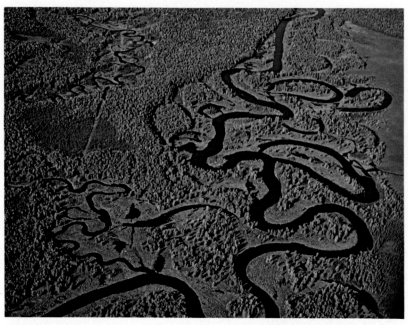

The "Little Su" has formed numerous oxbow lakes along its meandering course.

Aside from the upstream stretch, this river is a good floating stream for novices (from the George Parks Highway on). Sweepers and shallows demand alertness. The stream meanders intricately and is not recommended for the paddler impatient to reach the destination, but rather for those desiring a relaxing leisurely trip and for fishermen. Return by way of a prearranged chartered flight or by riverboat up Willow Creek.

River Location

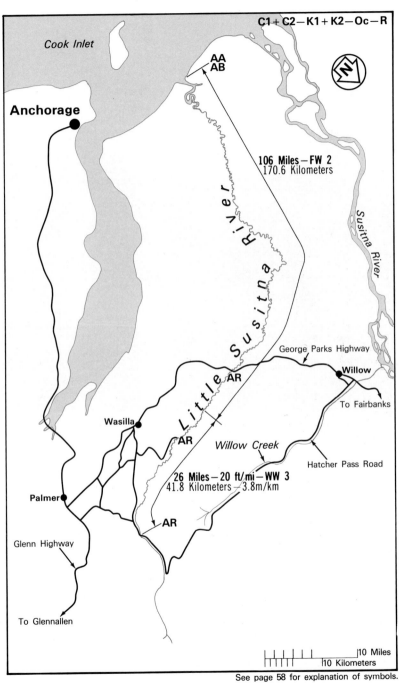

C1 + C2 − K1 + K2 − Oc − R

Cook Inlet

AA
AB

Anchorage

106 Miles — FW 2
170.6 Kilometers

Little Susitna River

Susitna River

George Parks Highway

Willow

AR

To Fairbanks

Wasilla

AR

Willow Creek

Hatcher Pass Road

26 Miles — 20 ft/mi — WW 3
41.8 Kilometers — 3.8m/km

Palmer

AR

Glenn Highway

To Glennallen

10 Miles
10 Kilometers

See page 58 for explanation of symbols.

14 Gulkana River

The Gulkana is one of the most popular white-water rivers in Alaska.

The Gulkana, one of the most popular white-water rivers in Alaska, is accessible by road at three points. Paxson Lake on the Richardson Highway is the starting point with a flat-water paddle across the lake to the river's outlet. About 18 miles downstream, there are falls with a portage on the left side. **For the next 8 miles through a canyon, there are difficult rapids that are for experienced paddlers only.** The rest of the river to Sourdough and on to Gulkana is moderately difficult, with many bends and high banks.

River Location

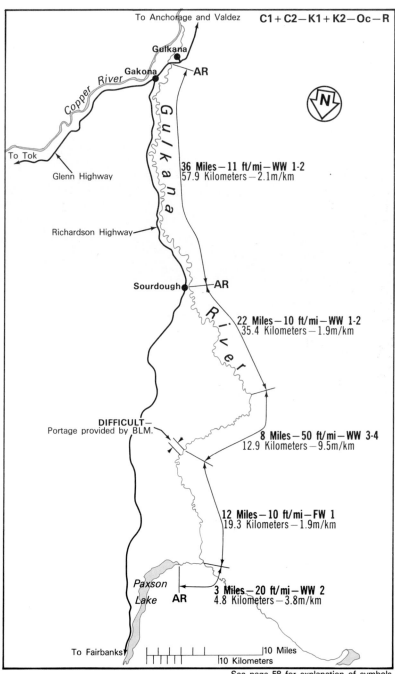

C1 + C2 − K1 + K2 − Oc − R

To Anchorage and Valdez

Gulkana

Gakona

AR

Copper River

To Tok

Glenn Highway

Gulkana

36 Miles — 11 ft/mi — WW 1-2
57.9 Kilometers — 2.1m/km

Richardson Highway

Sourdough

AR

River

22 Miles — 10 ft/mi — WW 1-2
35.4 Kilometers — 1.9m/km

DIFFICULT —
Portage provided by BLM.

8 Miles — 50 ft/mi — WW 3-4
12.9 Kilometers — 9.5m/km

12 Miles — 10 ft/mi — FW 1
19.3 Kilometers — 1.9m/km

Paxson
Lake

AR

3 Miles — 20 ft/mi — WW 2
4.8 Kilometers — 3.8m/km

To Fairbanks

10 Miles
10 Kilometers

See page 58 for explanation of symbols.

⑮ Copper River

The delta of the Copper River with Childs Glacier and Miles Lake in the Chugach Mountains.

Although the Richardson and Glenn Highways parallel the river, they are rarely within sight or sound of the stream. The braided river passes through true wilderness country and features about 200 miles of silty, but always swift water. The Copper flows by glacier-clad Mount Sanford, Mount Drum, Wrangell Peak and Mount Blackburn. Near Chitina, a gap opens through the Chugach Mountains to the Gulf of Alaska. No difficult white water is encountered along the way except at the end of Miles Lake, where the ice of Childs Glacier forms the western bank of the river. The powerful current frequently creates eddies and whirlpools of frightening dimensions. Once past Chitina, the next possible exit from the river is at a bridge on the Copper River Highway near the head of the delta on the gulf. A paddle into Cordova along the shore also is possible. Bird watchers will find a true abundance of migratory birds nesting on the Copper River flats.

River Location

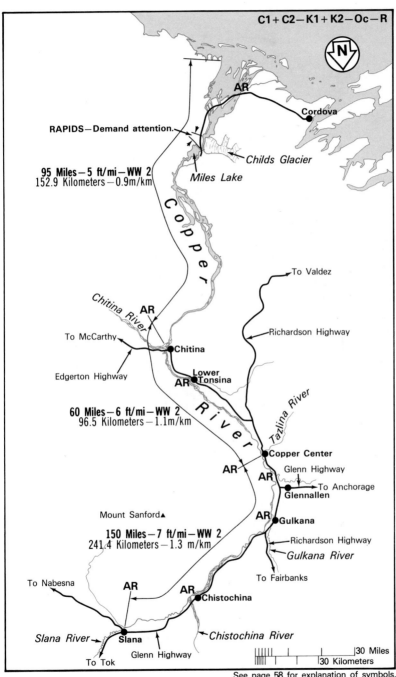

C1 + C2 – K1 + K2 – Oc – R

N

AR

Cordova

RAPIDS—Demand attention.

Childs Glacier

95 Miles – 5 ft/mi – WW 2
152.9 Kilometers – 0.9m/km

Miles Lake

Copper

To Valdez

Chitina River

AR

Richardson Highway

To McCarthy

Chitina

Edgerton Highway

Lower
Tonsina

AR

River

Tazlina River

60 Miles – 6 ft/mi – WW 2
96.5 Kilometers – 1.1m/km

Copper Center

AR

Glenn Highway

AR

To Anchorage

Glennallen

Mount Sanford▲

AR

Gulkana

150 Miles – 7 ft/mi – WW 2
241.4 Kilometers – 1.3 m/km

Richardson Highway

Gulkana River

To Fairbanks

To Nabesna

AR

AR

Chistochina

Slana River →

Slana

Chistochina River

Glenn Highway

30 Miles

30 Kilometers

To Tok

See page 58 for explanation of symbols.

16
Nabesna River

The Nabesna River is a small glacial stream that can be reached by the Nabesna Road, a beautiful route through high alpine country east of 16,237-foot Mount Sanford. The last miles to the river are a poor tractor trail; a four-wheel drive vehicle or a portage is necessary. The cold stream is in a wide graveled valley, and is braided and quite fast to start with. Eventually it slows to a river meandering through the foothills and taiga forest east of the Wrangell Mountains to the Alaska Highway near Northway Junction.

River Location

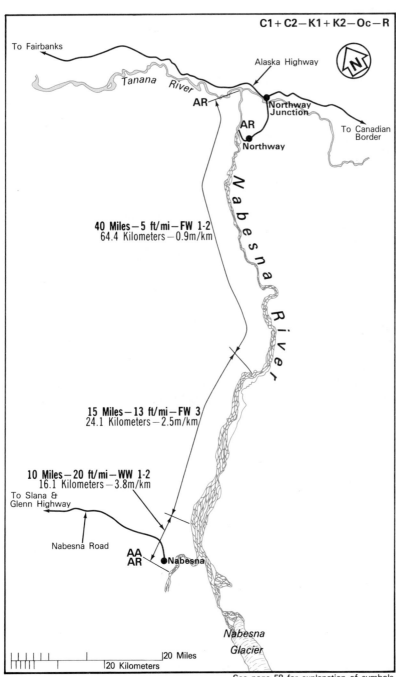

C1 + C2 − K1 + K2 − Oc − R

To Fairbanks

Tanana River

Alaska Highway

AR

AR

Northway Junction

Northway

To Canadian Border

Nabesna River

40 Miles − 5 ft/mi − FW 1-2
64.4 Kilometers − 0.9m/km

15 Miles − 13 ft/mi − FW 3
24.1 Kilometers − 2.5m/km

10 Miles − 20 ft/mi − WW 1-2
16.1 Kilometers − 3.8m/km

To Slana & Glenn Highway

Nabesna Road

AA
AR

Nabesna

Nabesna Glacier

20 Miles

20 Kilometers

See page 58 for explanation of symbols.

⑰ Klutina River

A party of kayakers makes a spring voyage on the Klutina.

Access to the Klutina River is possible with a four-wheel drive vehicle over a deplorably bad mud road to Klutina Lake or by aircraft. The river itself offers fantastic white-water paddling at low water volume. It is dangerous, if not impossible, at high water. Exit is possible at Copper Center before the Klutina enters the Copper River. The voyage may be continued on the Copper River to Chitina or to the Gulf of Alaska.

River Location

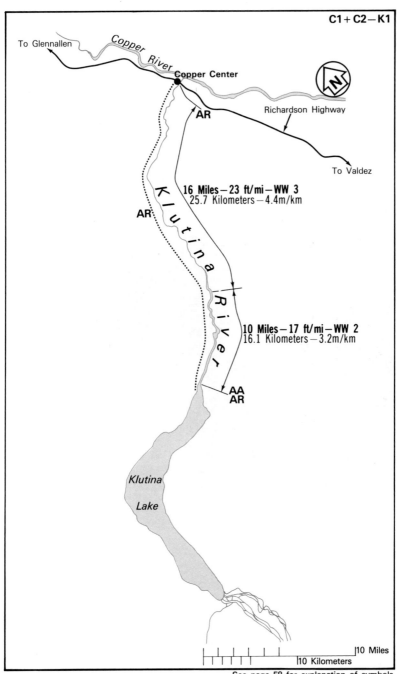

C1 + C2 – K1

To Glennallen

Copper River

Copper Center

AR

Richardson Highway

To Valdez

16 Miles – 23 ft/mi – WW 3
25.7 Kilometers – 4.4m/km

AR

Klutina River

10 Miles – 17 ft/mi – WW 2
16.1 Kilometers – 3.2m/km

AA
AR

Klutina Lake

10 Miles

10 Kilometers

See page 58 for explanation of symbols.

(18) Tonsina River

A tributary of the Copper, the Tonsina is a challenge for experienced white-water paddlers. **A very high water volume can make the river unsafe even for experienced paddlers.** The navigable portion of the Tonsina is shallow and braided along the upper section and is fast with a higher water volume along the lower section that flows through the forested Copper River Valley. The view on the upper river is dominated by mountains, the lower river by forests.

River Location

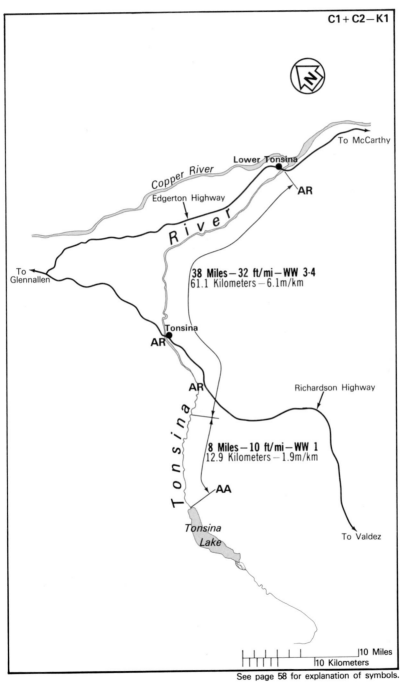

C1 + C2 — K1

To McCarthy

Lower Tonsina

Copper River

AR

Edgerton Highway

R i v e r

To Glennallen

38 Miles — 32 ft/mi — WW 3-4
61.1 Kilometers — 6.1m/km

Tonsina

AR

AR

Richardson Highway

8 Miles — 10 ft/mi — WW 1
12.9 Kilometers — 1.9m/km

T o n s i n a

AA

To Valdez

Tonsina
Lake

10 Miles

10 Kilometers

See page 58 for explanation of symbols.

19 Tazlina River

The Tazlina is a fast white-water river for experienced paddlers. Water volume must be judged carefully before embarking. The river is generally least difficult before spring runoff, in May and June, late in a dry summer or after cold weather slows glacial runoff. It is a rewarding trip for connoisseurs. Access is from the Glenn Highway via Little Nelchina River. Exit at a bridge on the Richardson Highway or continue on the Copper River.

River Location

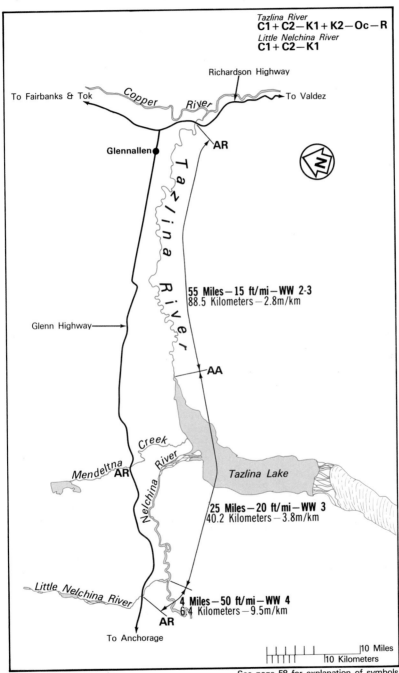

Tazlina River
C1 + C2 — K1 + K2 — Oc — R
Little Nelchina River
C1 + C2 — K1

Richardson Highway

To Fairbanks & Tok

Copper River

To Valdez

AR

Glennallen

N

Tazlina River

55 Miles — 15 ft/mi — WW 2-3
88.5 Kilometers — 2.8m/km

Glenn Highway

AA

Creek

Mendeltna

Nelchina River

AR

Tazlina Lake

25 Miles — 20 ft/mi — WW 3
40.2 Kilometers — 3.8m/km

Little Nelchina River

4 Miles — 50 ft/mi — WW 4
6.4 Kilometers — 9.5m/km

AR

To Anchorage

10 Miles
10 Kilometers

See page 58 for explanation of symbols.

⑳ Chitina River

The Chitina River is accessible by road with a four-wheel drive vehicle. Follow the extension of the Edgerton Highway from Chitina to McCarthy. **Experienced paddlers only may begin the trip on the Nizina, a tributary of the Chitina.** This 20-mile section of the Nizina has fairly fast water with difficult rapids. From the point where the Nizina joins it, the silty Chitina is a braided river with many gravel bars.

Access to the Chitina's glacial headwaters is possible by air charter, an option recommended for those who want to get into really wild mountain country on a fast, but not technically difficult, white-water river. Exit at Chitina below the highway bridge.

River Location

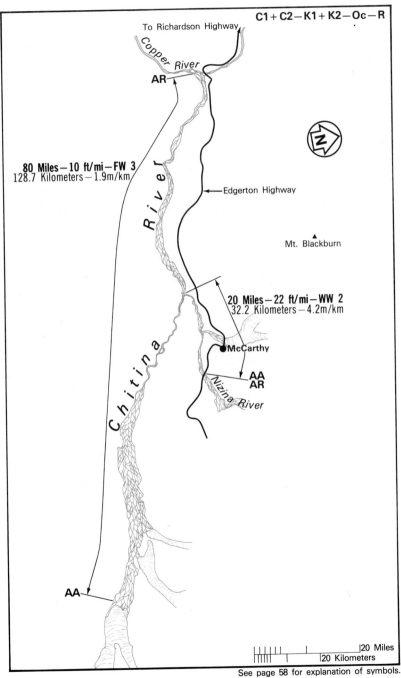

C1 + C2 — K1 + K2 — Oc — R

To Richardson Highway

Copper River

AR

80 Miles — 10 ft/mi — FW 3
128.7 Kilometers — 1.9m/km

River

Edgerton Highway

▲
Mt. Blackburn

20 Miles — 22 ft/mi — WW 2
32.2 Kilometers — 4.2m/km

McCarthy

AA
AR

Nizina River

Chitina

AA

20 Miles
20 Kilometers

See page 58 for explanation of symbols.

21
Alagnak River

A nice catch of king salmon can be an exciting bonus to a wilderness voyage on the Alagnak through Western Alaska.

With fishing and wildlife observation as attractions, the Alagnak River offers good rubber-raft trips. Some white water is an added bonus. As a white-water trip for kayaks or decked canoes, it is relatively short compared to the high cost of transportation to the starting point on the river. This trip combined with one to the Copper River of the Aleutian Range can make a terrific white-water vacation in Western Alaska.

River Location

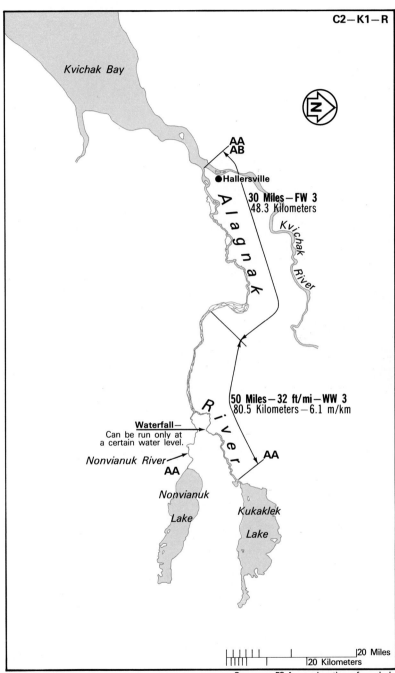

C2—K1—R

Kvichak Bay

AA
AB

●Hallersville

30 Miles—FW 3
48.3 Kilometers

Kvichak River

A l a g n a k

50 Miles—32 ft/mi—WW 3
80.5 Kilometers—6.1 m/km

R i v e r

Waterfall—
Can be run only at
a certain water level.

Nonvianuk River

AA

AA

Nonvianuk
Lake

Kukaklek
Lake

|20 Miles
|20 Kilometers

See page 58 for explanation of symbols.

㉒ Togiak River

A trip down this beautiful river through Western Alaska tundra country to the Bering Sea is a special delight for ardent fishermen. Begin at Upper Togiak Lake. The most interesting scenery is along the stretch of river between this lake and Togiak Lake. Fishing is superb. Brown bears know it too, so be alert.

River Location

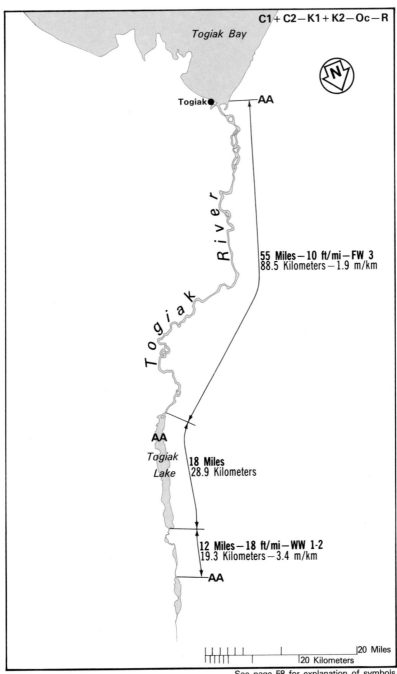

C1 + C2 — K1 + K2 — Oc — R

Togiak Bay

Togiak● AA

Togiak River

55 Miles — 10 ft/mi — FW 3
88.5 Kilometers — 1.9 m/km

AA
Togiak Lake

18 Miles
28.9 Kilometers

12 Miles — 18 ft/mi — WW 1-2
19.3 Kilometers — 3.4 m/km

AA

20 Miles
20 Kilometers

See page 58 for explanation of symbols.

(23) Copper River

In the Aleutian Range

Boaters visiting Western Alaska should not miss this fast, clear-water river. It may be too short to justify the expense of flying into the area, but fishing is superb and the white-water thrill is all there. It's a good river to travel on a raft excursion. Eight miles above its mouth there are three falls, one of which must be portaged.

River Location

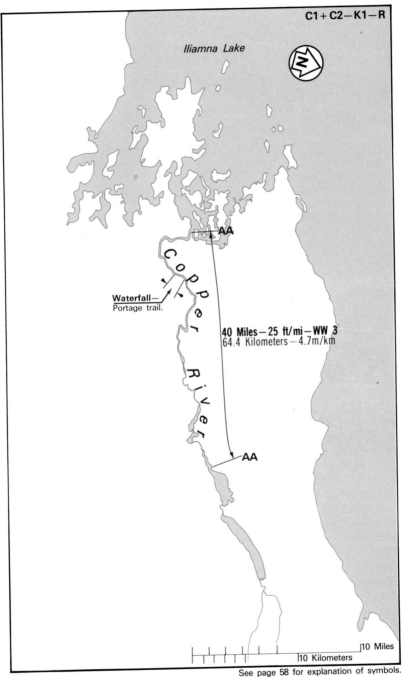

Kuskokwim River

The North Fork reaches far north to the Tanana basin. It served as an ancient watercourse for Natives, and later was used by prospectors and trappers. Lake Minchumina is connected by a long, once well-trod portage to the North Fork. There are few travelers today, so modern voyagers must be prepared to rely on their own resources. The first village reached, Medfra, is located where the East Fork merges with the North Fork. From that point on, the Kuskokwim is a wide river, flowing slowly through mountains to the broad coastal plain. The largest settlements are McGrath, Sleetmute, Russian Mission, Aniak, and Bethel at the river's mouth. Each village has its riverboat fleet. This is moose country.

River Location

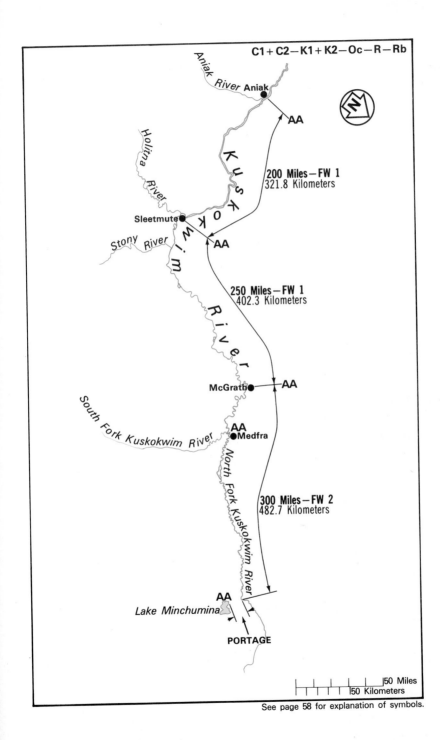

C1 + C2 — K1 + K2 — Oc — R — Rb

Aniak River

Aniak

AA

Kuskokwim

Holitna River

200 Miles — FW 1
321.8 Kilometers

Sleetmute

Stony River

AA

River

250 Miles — FW 1
402.3 Kilometers

McGrath

AA

South Fork Kuskokwim River

AA
Medfra

North Fork Kuskokwim River

300 Miles — FW 2
482.7 Kilometers

AA
Lake Minchumina

PORTAGE

|50 Miles
|50 Kilometers

See page 58 for explanation of symbols.

(25) Holitna River

Now seldom visited, the Holitna River in the Kuskokwim basin once saw much activity. It is a slow taiga river that served as the Russians' first route into the Interior from Bristol Bay.

The river poses no technical problems, but there is always the danger of sweepers and logjams. Fishing is fair when the water is not muddied by heavy rain. **Only travelers with prior wilderness experience should attempt this isolated river.**

River Location

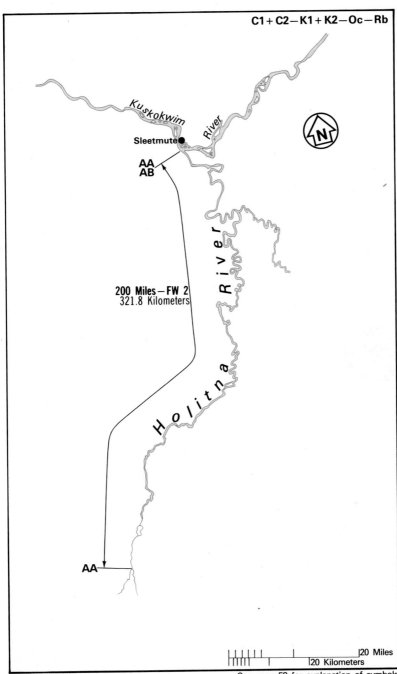

C1+C2−K1+K2−Oc−Rb

Kuskokwim River

Sleetmute

AA
AB

200 Miles − FW 2
321.8 Kilometers

Holitna River

N

AA

20 Miles
20 Kilometers

See page 58 for explanation of symbols.

(26)

Stony River

The Stony River has become a popular float trip for hunters. Travelers who come only to sightsee should plan their trip before hunting season opens. The first 2-days' travel from Telaquana Lake is on fast water. The river then steadies to a slower, but still brisk pace. For an easy float, fly in to the river below the junction of the main fork and the Telaquana River. Exit is possible at Stony River village on the Kuskokwim, or continue on to one of the larger villages.

River Location

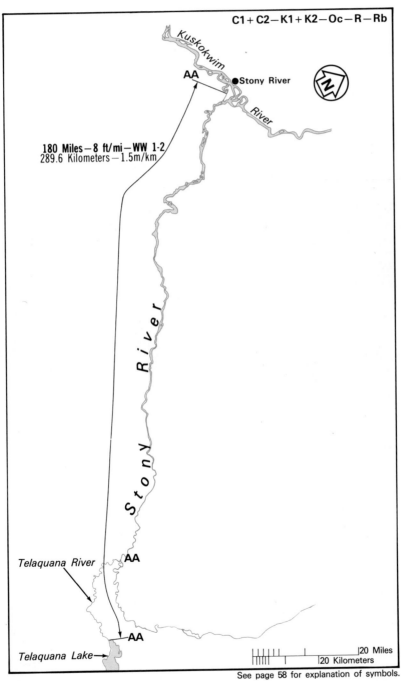

C1 + C2 — K1 + K2 — Oc — R — Rb

Kuskokwim

AA

●Stony River

River

N

180 Miles — 8 ft/mi — WW 1-2
289.6 Kilometers — 1.5m/km

S t o n y   R i v e r

Telaquana River

AA

AA

Telaquana Lake →

20 Miles
20 Kilometers

See page 58 for explanation of symbols.

㉗ Tikchik River

The Tikchik River can form the first leg of a highly recommended voyage from the Ahklun Mountains to Bristol Bay.

A clear, gravelly stream, the Tikchik River has superb fishing with ptarmigan, migratory birds, beavers and bears on its islands and banks. Fast, with sweepers but no rapids, it is an excellent river for the fisherman to drift. The push-off point at Nishlik Lake can be reached by chartering an airplane from Dillingham. Exit at Tikchik Lake, where there is a fishing lodge. A continuation on the Nuyakuk River to the Nushagak River makes this trip one of the most highly recommended voyages in Western Alaska, especially for the ardent fisherman.

River Location

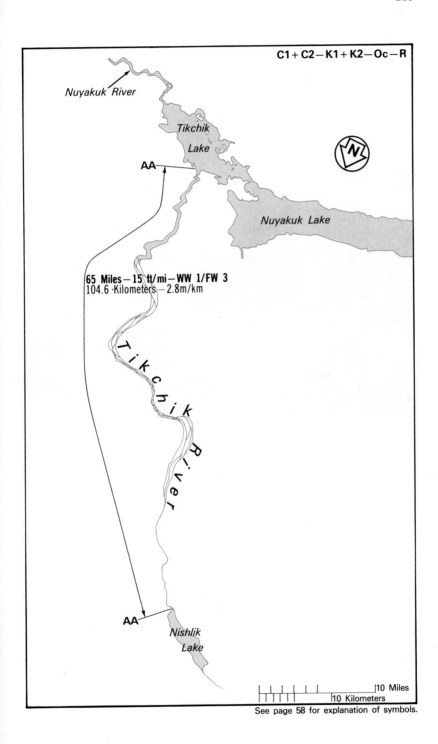

C1 + C2 — K1 + K2 — Oc — R

Nuyakuk River

Tikchik Lake

AA

Nuyakuk Lake

65 Miles — 15 ft/mi — WW 1/FW 3
104.6 Kilometers — 2.8m/km

Tikchik River

AA

Nishlik Lake

10 Miles
10 Kilometers

See page 58 for explanation of symbols.

(28) Aniak River

Sweepers are a constant threat on the Aniak at high water.

The Aniak is a river with three distinctly different phases. There is a clear, gravelly section from the lake near its head through the forest and into the tundra. The second phase begins where the course disintegrates into many channels, filled with an abundance of sweepers, logjams and uprooted trees. Below this very difficult stretch, the water becomes tame. It is riverboat country, flat water all the way to Aniak on the Kuskokwim. The Aniak River should be attempted only by the most experienced wilderness travelers.

River Location

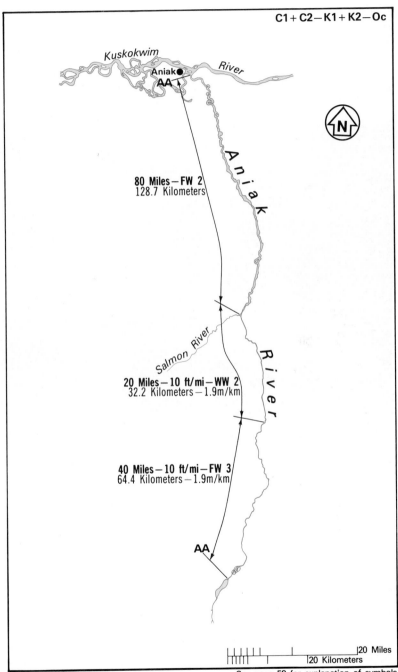

See page 58 for explanation of symbols.

㉙ Chilikadrotna River

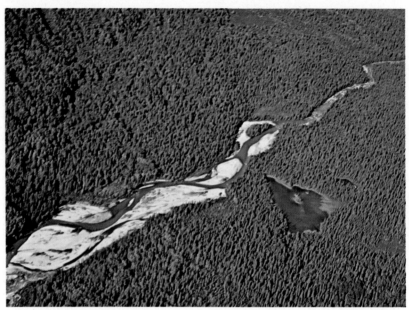

The Chilikadrotna, flowing through the forests west of the Aleutian Range, demands much, even of experienced paddlers.

A very enchanting river in the forested area west of the Aleutian Range, the Chilikadrotna is demanding, even of experienced paddlers and wilderness travelers. It has many stretches of fast water and rapids. Fishing is superb for grayling, rainbow and pike. Fly out from the Mulchatna River or from one of the villages on the Nushagak River.

River Location

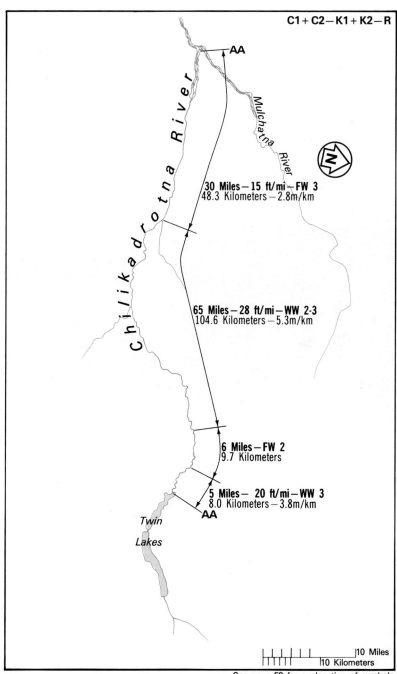

C1 + C2 — K1 + K2 — R

Mulchatna River

Chilikadrotna River

AA

30 Miles — 15 ft/mi — FW 3
48.3 Kilometers — 2.8m/km

65 Miles — 28 ft/mi — WW 2-3
104.6 Kilometers — 5.3m/km

6 Miles — FW 2
9.7 Kilometers

5 Miles — 20 ft/mi — WW 3
8.0 Kilometers — 3.8m/km
AA

Twin Lakes

10 Miles
10 Kilometers

See page 58 for explanation of symbols.

㉚ Nushagak River

Brigitte on the Nushagak River at the village of Ekwok where fish are drying on racks in the sun.

The Nushagak was the first river in this area ascended by the Russians (early 1800's). Much of the river's course is fringed by scattered forests, but the tundra is never very far away. The headwaters drain the Taylor Mountains, while the major tributaries, the Nuyakuk River and the Mulchatna River, carry drainage from the lake country in the west and glaciers in the east. The upper course is very remote. As with most rivers that flow through forests, sweepers and logjams are the major obstacles. Fishing is good.

River Location

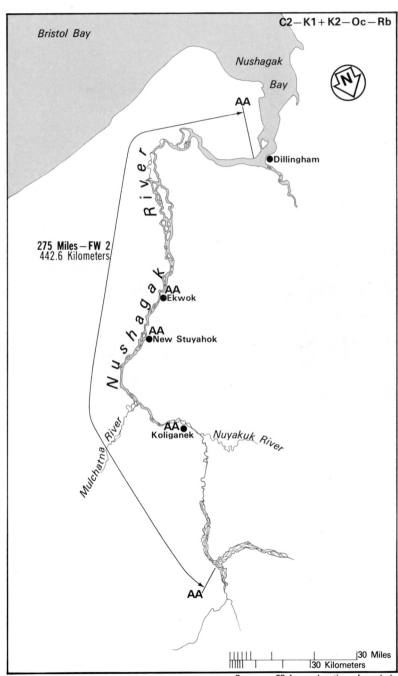

See page 58 for explanation of symbols.

③① Mulchatna River

Foldboats are widely used on remote rivers like the Mulchatna.

The Mulchatna is a fine river that flows through the tundra country of Western Alaska. Portions of the river valley are swampy, but there are many high places for attractive camp-sites. Fishing is superb. Wildlife includes a large beaver population. Downstream from Turquoise Lake there is fast water. Otherwise, the river is flat water with the ever-present danger of unexpected sweepers or log-jams in one of the channels or branches.

River Location

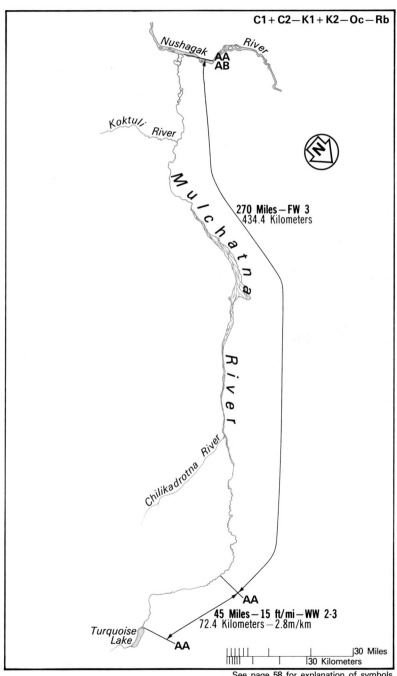

C1 + C2 — K1 + K2 — Oc — Rb

Nushagak River

AA
AB

Koktuli River

Mulchatna River

270 Miles — FW 3
434.4 Kilometers

Chilikadrotna River

AA

45 Miles — 15 ft/mi — WW 2-3
72.4 Kilometers — 2.8m/km

Turquoise Lake

AA

30 Miles
30 Kilometers

See page 58 for explanation of symbols.

Nuyakuk River

This river combines a terrific fishing trip with an outstanding river voyage. Below Tikchik Lake there is one waterfall that must be portaged. Otherwise, the river poses no technical challenges, but it does pass through wild country. Bear, beaver and an occasional caribou may be encountered.

River Location

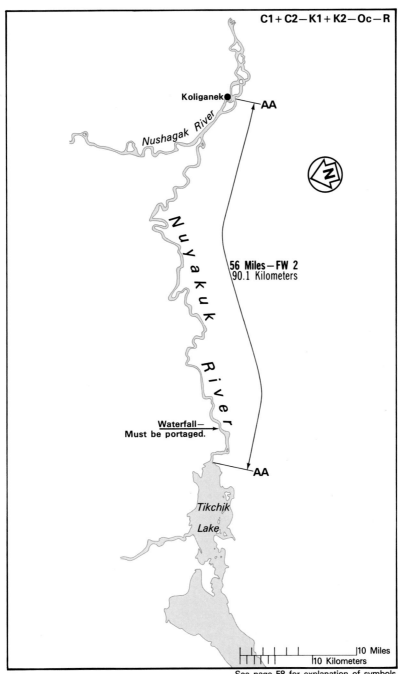

C1 + C2 − K1 + K2 − Oc − R

Koliganek● →AA

Nushagak River

N u y a k u k   R i v e r

56 Miles — FW 2
90.1 Kilometers

Waterfall —
Must be portaged. →

→AA

Tikchik
Lake

|10 Miles
|10 Kilometers

See page 58 for explanation of symbols.

Porcupine River

Golden leaves signal the approach of winter along the historic Porcupine River.

The Porcupine River is the perfect route to satisfy a modern-day voyager. The remote wilderness and rich historic past of the river offer a rewarding experience of lasting value. Difficulties along the river are minor, so the trip is suitable for families with older children. Access can be made by chartering an airplane to the upper Porcupine or to Summit Lake on the Bell River. Voyagers must check with U.S. Customs and Immigration Services in either Fairbanks or Anchorage on their return, as the point of origin is in Canada.

River Location

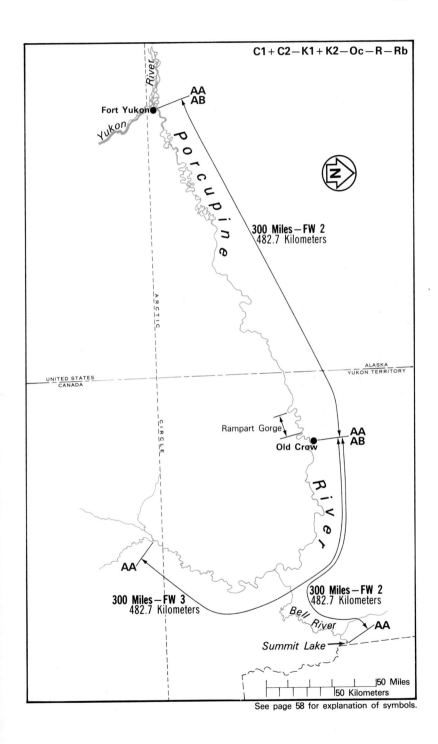

C1 + C2 — K1 + K2 — Oc — R — Rb

AA
AB

Fort Yukon

Yukon

River

Porcupine

300 Miles — FW 2
482.7 Kilometers

ARCTIC

UNITED STATES
CANADA

ALASKA
YUKON TERRITORY

Rampart Gorge

Old Crow

AA
AB

River

CIRCLE

AA

300 Miles — FW 3
482.7 Kilometers

300 Miles — FW 2
482.7 Kilometers

Bell River

AA

Summit Lake

50 Miles

50 Kilometers

See page 58 for explanation of symbols.

(34) Sheenjek River

A popular river on the southern slope of the Brooks Range, the Sheenjek is remote and usually is a slow-flowing river. At times of high water, however, it becomes a raging torrent that must be approached with care. Most of its length is through the arctic taiga.

River Location

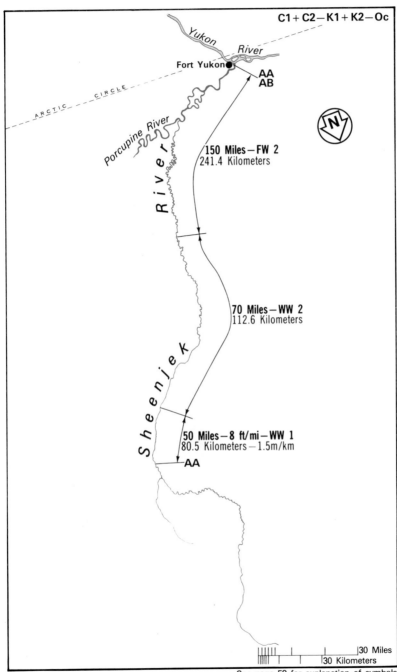

See page 58 for explanation of symbols.

(35) Koyukuk River

For those who would combine drifting, occasional Native settlements and wildlife, the Koyukuk is a choice river. A voyage can be stretched all the way to the Bering Sea. Any settlement is a potential starting point, but Wiseman, once a mining town, is the most practical northern starting point. The river normally does not present any significant difficulties.

River Location

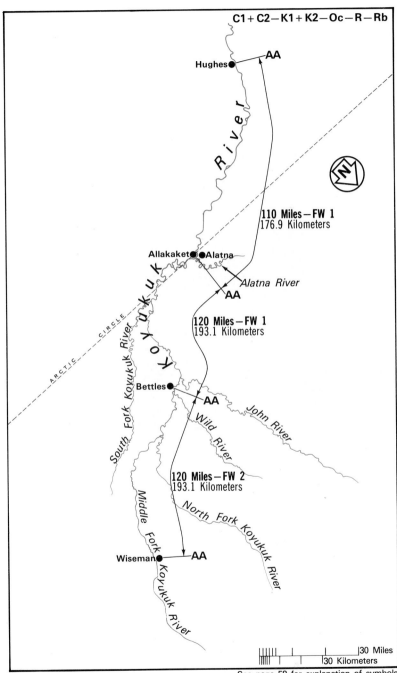

C1+C2−K1+K2−Oc−R−Rb

Hughes● →AA

River

110 Miles−FW 1
176.9 Kilometers

Allakaket●●Alatna

Alatna River
←AA

Koyukuk

120 Miles−FW 1
193.1 Kilometers

South Fork Koyukuk River

ARCTIC CIRCLE

Bettles●
AA

Wild River
John River

120 Miles−FW 2
193.1 Kilometers

Middle Fork
North Fork Koyukuk River

Wiseman● →AA

Koyukuk River

30 Miles
30 Kilometers

See page 58 for explanation of symbols.

(36) John River

A short hike offers a commanding view of the John River and the Endicott Mountains.

The John River makes a rewarding voyage for the adventuresome traveler. It is possible to paddle the length of the river by starting at the Eskimo village of Anaktuvuk Pass. A short portage and lining on the small creek near the village is necessary. **Experience is essential for safe negotiation of some upstream fast water and easy rapids.**

River Location

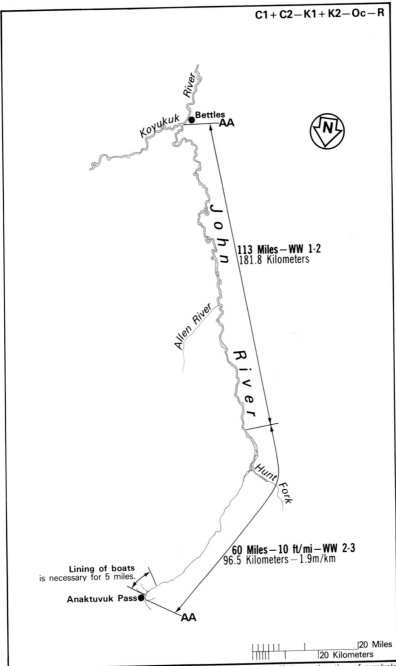

C1 + C2 − K1 + K2 − Oc − R

Koyukuk River

Bettles
AA

John River

113 Miles — WW 1-2
181.8 Kilometers

Allen River

Hunt Fork

60 Miles — 10 ft/mi — WW 2-3
96.5 Kilometers — 1.9m/km

Lining of boats
is necessary for 5 miles.

Anaktuvuk Pass
AA

20 Miles
20 Kilometers

See page 58 for explanation of symbols.

㊲ Wild River

A tributary of the Koyukuk, the Wild River is recommended for enthusiasts of meandering streams. It flows from Wild Lake to the Koyukuk. Spending some time on the lake, then drifting the river will give voyagers ample opportunities to fish and observe wildlife. Access is possible by chartering a plane to Wild Lake. Exit on the Koyukuk River.

River Location

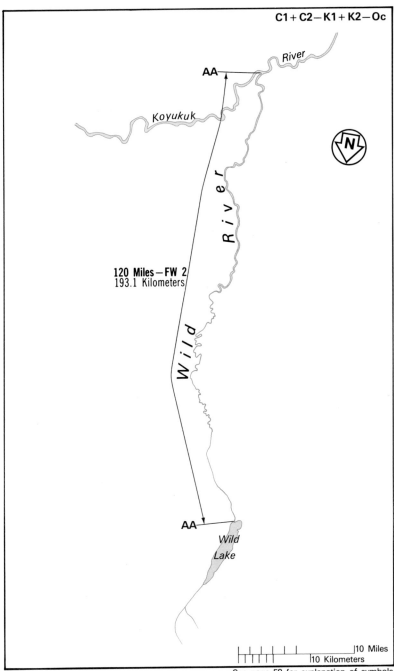

C1 + C2 — K1 + K2 — Oc

River

AA

Koyukuk

R i v e r

N

120 Miles — FW 2
193.1 Kilometers

W i l d

AA

Wild
Lake

10 Miles
10 Kilometers

See page 58 for explanation of symbols.

38

Anaktuvuk River

The Anaktuvuk is a small river with swift, clear waters. From Anaktuvuk Pass, a settlement in the broad pass famous for its caribou migration, it's a short portage over a good path to Cache Lake. From there a small stream flows to the Anaktuvuk River. After a few miles of fast water, the Anaktuvuk meanders slowly for 30 miles through a valley between the arctic foothills. As the river passes from the hills into the flat tundra country, it quickens, and a section of rapids, braided shallows and fast water provide a challenging day or two. The last 40 miles to the juncture with the Colville River have no major rapids but do feature very fast water and sharply defined eddies.

River Location

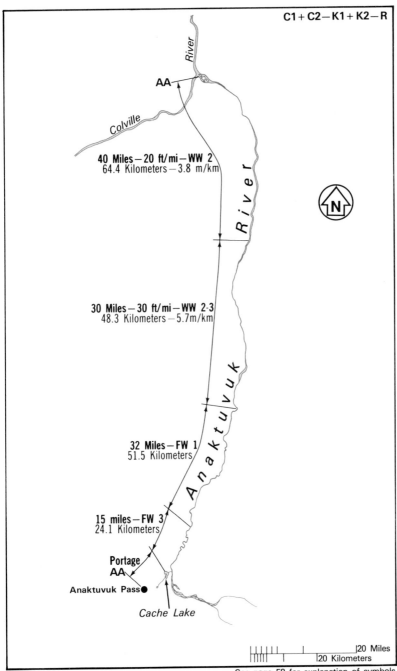

C1 + C2 − K1 + K2 − R

AA

River

Colville

40 Miles — 20 ft/mi — WW 2
64.4 Kilometers — 3.8 m/km

River

N

30 Miles — 30 ft/mi — WW 2-3
48.3 Kilometers — 5.7m/km

Anaktuvuk

32 Miles — FW 1
51.5 Kilometers

15 miles — FW 3
24.1 Kilometers

Portage
AA

Anaktuvuk Pass

Cache Lake

]20 Miles
]20 Kilometers

See page 58 for explanation of symbols.

Chandalar River

The Chandalar is an exciting, interesting river. Below the confluence of the North and East Fork Chandalar rivers, it is quite fast and never dull. Both forks flow through forested areas on the south slope of the Brooks Range. Glaciers associated with the rivers should be reconnoitered carefully. The Junjik River, above Arctic Village, is a challenging option for white-water paddlers. The upper East Fork Chandalar River is very fast but not spiked with rapids. The more difficult North Fork flows through Chandalar Lake. The Chandalar itself is a placid river. The East Fork serves as the boundary of the Chandalar Indian Reservation.

River Location

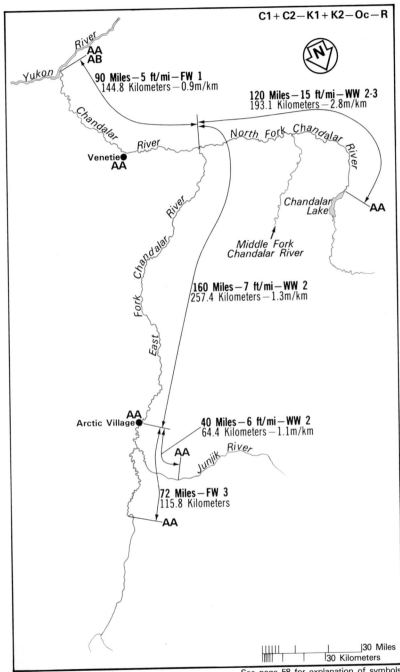

C1 + C2 — K1 + K2 — Oc — R

AA
AB

90 Miles — 5 ft/mi — FW 1
144.8 Kilometers — 0.9m/km

120 Miles — 15 ft/mi — WW 2-3
193.1 Kilometers — 2.8m/km

Yukon River

Chandalar River

North Fork Chandalar River

Venetie
AA

River

Chandalar
Lake

AA

Chandalar Fork

Middle Fork
Chandalar River

160 Miles — 7 ft/mi — WW 2
257.4 Kilometers — 1.3m/km

East

AA
Arctic Village

40 Miles — 6 ft/mi — WW 2
64.4 Kilometers — 1.1m/km

AA

Junjik River

72 Miles — FW 3
115.8 Kilometers

AA

30 Miles

30 Kilometers

See page 58 for explanation of symbols.

40 Nigu River

Towering mountains dominate the Nigu River, one of the least visited waterways in the Brooks Range.

The Nigu River probably is one of the least visited waterways in the Brooks Range. **It is only for experienced paddlers and wilderness travelers.** Access is possible by chartered plane to a small lake at the head of the Nigu and Alatna River valleys. Boats must be lined the first few miles. Then it is possible to proceed cautiously down the narrow course of the fast, shallow stream. The Nigu meanders through high mountains, as it flows northwest to the Etivluk River. Rapids spike some of the lower sections of the stream.

River Location

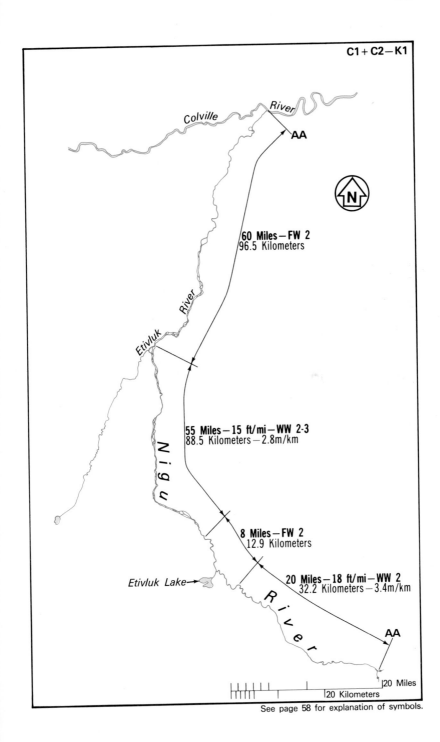

C1 + C2 — K1

Colville   River

AA

N

60 Miles — FW 2
96.5 Kilometers

Etivluk   River

N i g u

55 Miles — 15 ft/mi — WW 2-3
88.5 Kilometers — 2.8m/km

8 Miles — FW 2
12.9 Kilometers

Etivluk Lake

20 Miles — 18 ft/mi — WW 2
32.2 Kilometers — 3.4m/km

R i v e r

AA

20 Miles
20 Kilometers

See page 58 for explanation of symbols.

Aniuk River

The Aniuk flows south from the Brooks Range to the Noatak River.

Very remote and rarely traveled, the Aniuk is a small, interesting river in the Brooks Range. It is highly recommended as a side trip or as a starting point for the Noatak River. It alone might not justify the time and cost of a trip. In dry years, the Aniuk is quite shallow but still navigable.

River Location

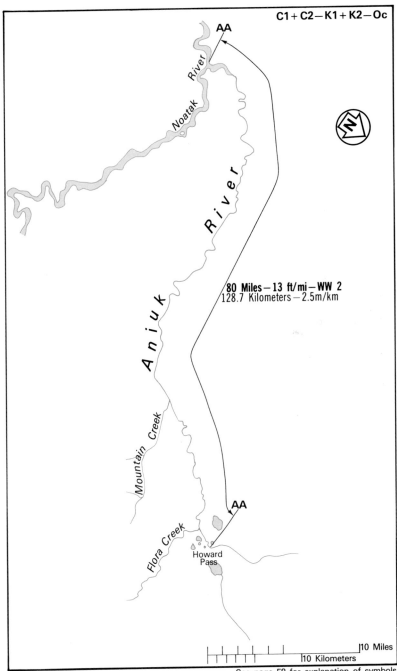

C1 + C2 — K1 + K2 — Oc

AA

Noatak River

A n i u k   R i v e r

80 Miles — 13 ft/mi — WW 2
128.7 Kilometers — 2.5m/km

Mountain Creek

AA

Flora Creek

Howard
Pass

10 Miles

10 Kilometers

See page 58 for explanation of symbols.

(42) Killik River

Probably the best known of the North Slope rivers, the Killik flows through caribou and wolf country. Access is best at the joining of April and Easter creeks. About halfway to the Colville River there are rapids that should be inspected before passage is attempted.

River Location

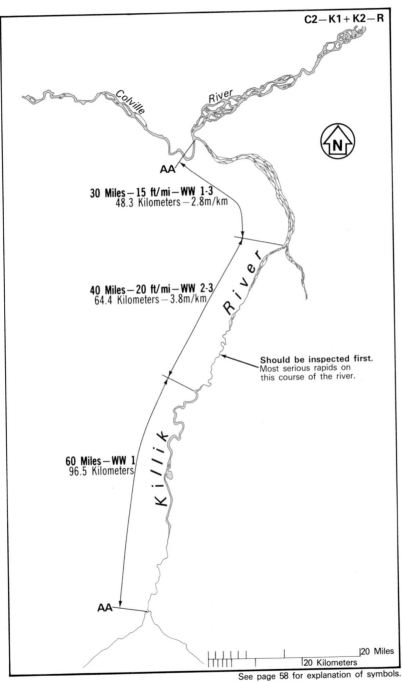

C2 — K1 + K2 — R

Colville River

N

AA

30 Miles — 15 ft/mi — WW 1-3
48.3 Kilometers — 2.8m/km

40 Miles — 20 ft/mi — WW 2-3
64.4 Kilometers — 3.8m/km

River

Should be inspected first.
Most serious rapids on
this course of the river.

Killik

60 Miles — WW 1
96.5 Kilometers

AA

20 Miles

20 Kilometers

See page 58 for explanation of symbols.

43 Colville River

By far the largest of the rivers on the north slope of the Brooks Range, the Colville bisects the arctic plain as it flows north into Harrison Bay on the Arctic Ocean. Except for the feeders, Thunder and Storm creeks at its head, the Colville is not a difficult river to run. **Only experienced voyagers should venture into this river because of its remoteness.**

River Location

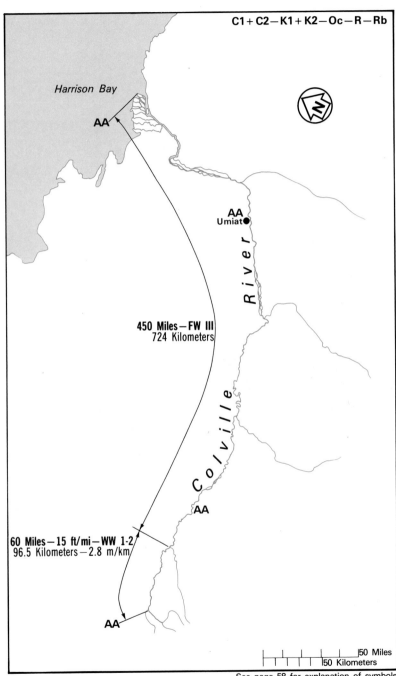

C1 + C2 − K1 + K2 − Oc − R − Rb

Harrison Bay

AA

AA
Umiat

River

450 Miles − FW III
724 Kilometers

Colville

AA

60 Miles − 15 ft/mi − WW 1-2
96.5 Kilometers − 2.8 m/km

AA

50 Miles
50 Kilometers

See page 58 for explanation of symbols.

44 Noatak River

Entirely above the Arctic Circle, the Noatak is one of Alaska's finest wild rivers.

Some consider the Noatak the finest wild river in the Arctic. It flows through forest and tundra, and is entirely above the Arctic Circle. Highlights of travel on this river are the mountain section, Noatak Canyon and the run to the coast below the village of Noatak. In the clear section of the river, fishing for grayling is excellent.

River Location

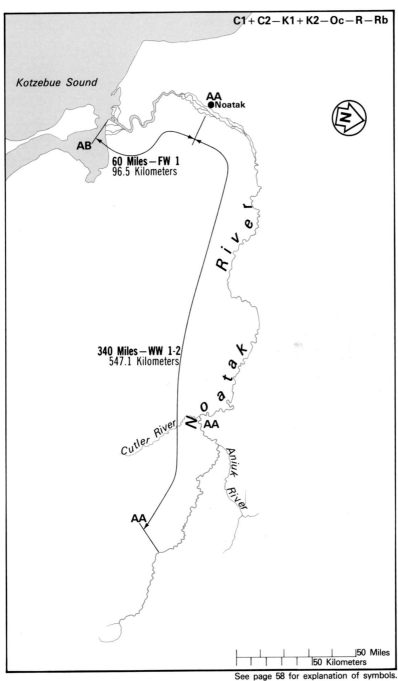

C1 + C2 — K1 + K2 — Oc — R — Rb

Kotzebue Sound

AA
●Noatak

AB

60 Miles — FW 1
96.5 Kilometers

River

340 Miles — WW 1-2
547.1 Kilometers

Noatak

Cutler River   AA

Aniuk River

AA

50 Miles
50 Kilometers

See page 58 for explanation of symbols.

45

Kobuk River

The Kobuk poses no particular difficulties other than the rapids near its headwaters at Walker Lake.

The Kobuk was probably the first river in the Brooks Range discovered and traveled by explorers. Several villages are situated along its banks. Access is possible to the villages by scheduled air service or to Walker Lake by charter. The first few miles out of Walker Lake include some difficult rapids. Lining and/or portaging around the rapids is recommended. Otherwise, the river poses no particular difficulties. The Kobuk offers rich rewards to voyagers with time and patience. Wildlife includes moose, bear, caribou and wolf.

River Location

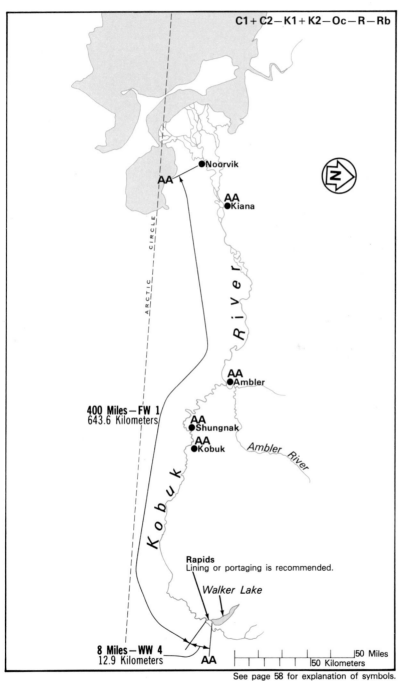

C1 + C2 — K1 + K2 — Oc — R — Rb

●Noorvik

AA

AA
●Kiana

ARCTIC CIRCLE

River

AA
●Ambler

400 Miles — FW 1
643.6 Kilometers

AA
●Shungnak

AA
●Kobuk

Ambler River

Kobuk

Rapids
Lining or portaging is recommended.

Walker Lake

8 Miles — WW 4
12.9 Kilometers

AA

|50 Miles

|50 Kilometers

See page 58 for explanation of symbols.

(46) Redstone River, Cutler River

From the Kobuk River to the Noatak River

This traverse allows wilderness travelers to cross some extremely remote country and to connect two major river systems with a comparatively short portage. The south-north traverse from the village of Ambler to the Redstone River is recommended. The Redstone is slow enough to permit upstream paddling and easy lining. An obvious low valley opening indicates one possible route for the portage. A second possible portage, a shorter route, is through the next valley, about 6 miles upriver. The Cutler River, a clear, shallow stream with a string of easy rapids is just over the divide from the Redstone. Continuing down the Noatak duplicates an old Eskimo hunting expedition route. The traverse in the opposite direction, from the Cutler to the Redstone, also is possible but involves a longer upstream paddle and more lining.

River Location

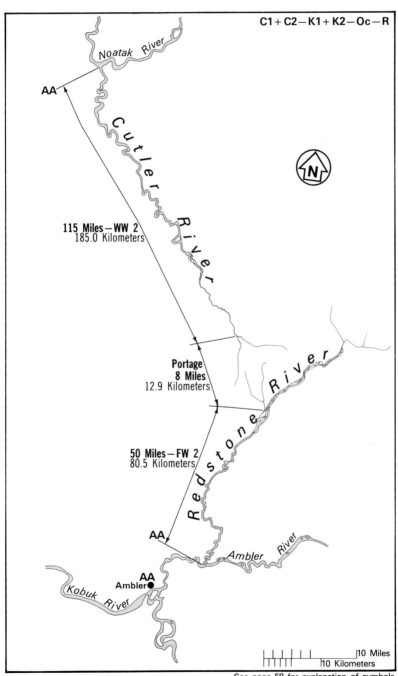

C1 + C2 — K1 + K2 — Oc — R

Noatak River

AA

Cutler River

115 Miles — WW 2
185.0 Kilometers

Portage
8 Miles
12.9 Kilometers

Redstone River

50 Miles — FW 2
80.5 Kilometers

AA

Ambler River

AA
Ambler●

Kobuk River

10 Miles
10 Kilometers

See page 58 for explanation of symbols.

47 Ambler River

A summer's night on the Ambler River is softly lit by the midnight sun.

The Ambler is a small, clear river flowing through the forests of the Brooks Range. It makes a terrific wilderness voyage, either by itself, or as the beginning of a longer trip. A crossover from the Noatak River also is possible. Sweepers are a danger on the upper Ambler, as is a difficult 3-mile canyon at high water. **Only experienced wilderness travelers should attempt this voyage.** Grayling are abundant. Exit is possible at the village of Ambler.

River Location

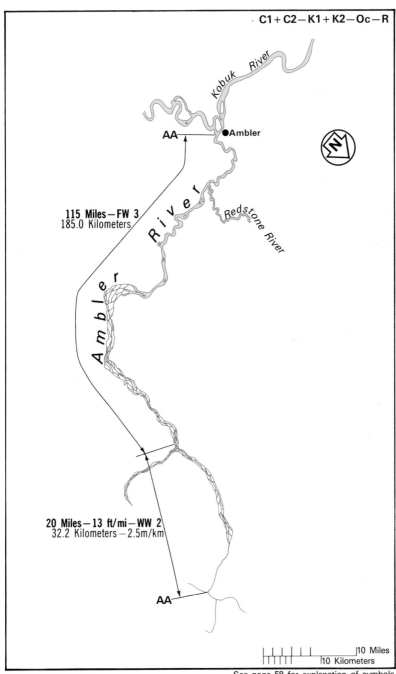

C1 + C2 — K1 + K2 — Oc — R

Kobuk River

●Ambler

AA

Ambler River

Redstone River

115 Miles — FW 3
185.0 Kilometers

20 Miles — 13 ft/mi — WW 2
32.2 Kilometers — 2.5m/km

AA

10 Miles
10 Kilometers

See page 58 for explanation of symbols.

Alatna River

The Alatna River meanders through a forested valley on the southern slope of the Brooks Range. The area is famous for the granite spires of the Arrigetch Peaks to the west. Highly advanced paddling skills are not required on this trip, but the country is a remote wilderness. The Alatna flows slowly, offering the voyager time to enjoy the scenery. Exit is possible from either Alatna or Allakaket. Continuing down the Koyukuk can extend the voyage.

River Location

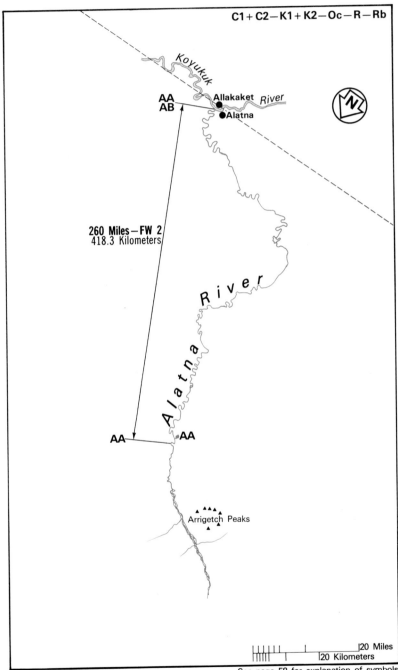

C1 + C2 − K1 + K2 − Oc − R − Rb

Koyukuk

AA
AB
Allakaket _River_
●Alatna

260 Miles − FW 2
418.3 Kilometers

Alatna River

AA ⊦ AA

▲▲▲▲
Arrigetch Peaks
▲ ▲

|20 Miles
20 Kilometers

See page 58 for explanation of symbols.

Kantishna River

The Kantishna is a historic route between the Tanana and the Kuskokwim basins (via the Lake Minchumina portage). Many prospectors and trappers traveled up the river, summer and winter, to work their claims or traplines along the foothills of Mount McKinley. The river is not difficult. It meanders and flows slowly through the forests of Interior Alaska. More skillful paddlers may wish to try an alternate route on the tributary stream, Moose Creek. It has some rapids and shallow stretches in dry seasons.

River
Location

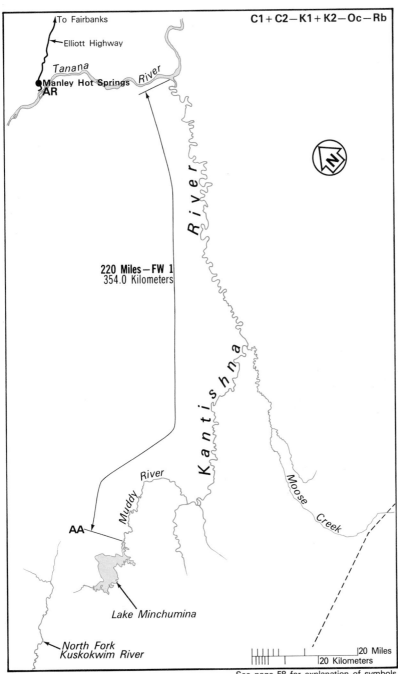

C1 + C2 − K1 + K2 − Oc − Rb

To Fairbanks

Elliott Highway

Tanana

Manley Hot Springs

AR

River

River

220 Miles − FW 1
354.0 Kilometers

Kantishna

Muddy River

Moose Creek

AA

Lake Minchumina

North Fork
Kuskokwim River

20 Miles

20 Kilometers

See page 58 for explanation of symbols.

Tanana River

The glacial-fed Tanana is silty and braided.

A mighty tributary of the Yukon River, the Tanana is navigable for its full length and gives travelers many options. The Alaska Highway, the George Parks Highway and the Elliott Highway all have access to the Tanana. The Tanana is a sprawling river with many channels and islands. Paddlers of small craft must be alert for drifting trees, logjams and whirlpools. Avoid the flood period, late June through early July. The river enters the Yukon at Tanana.

River Location

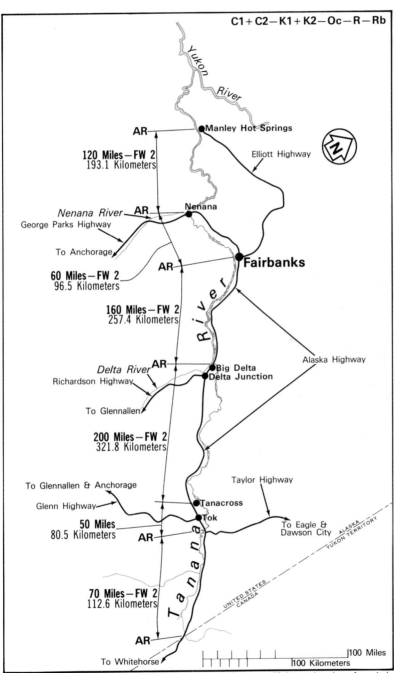

See page 58 for explanation of symbols.

51

Alsek River

One of the most spectacular river breakthroughs in North America is the Alsek as it cuts its bed out of the Saint Elias Mountains. **Flanked by towering mountains and hemmed in by glaciers, this DANGEROUS river is no place for the casual river runner, even if technically proficient.** Tweedsmuir Glacier must be crossed for over 10 miles to portage around the unnavigable Turnback Canyon. Now, certain glacial conditions even can make this route unfeasible. The 150-mile section above Tweedsmuir Glacier is difficult white water having high water volume and velocity. After the long, difficult portage, the river still demands respect, but the difficulties occur at a lower rate. High winds and wandering grizzlies are other hazards to be reckoned with. After passing more river-level glaciers, the Alsek merges with the Pacific Ocean in the Gulf of Alaska at Dry Bay. There fishermen can radio either Yakutat or Juneau for air transportation. To my knowledge, only three parties have traveled the whole length of the river. It is a major undertaking, not to be considered lightly.

River Location

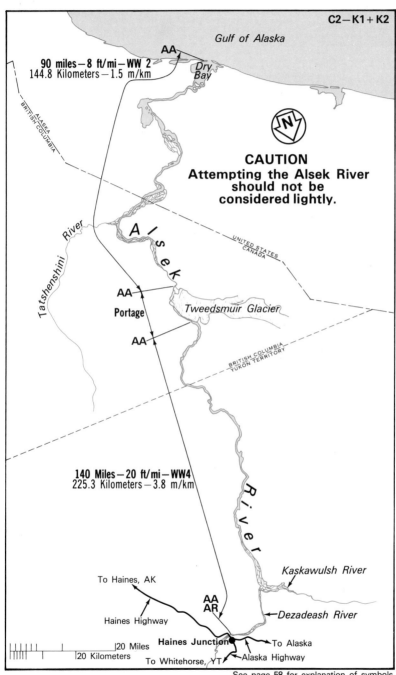

C2−K1+K2

Gulf of Alaska

90 miles−8 ft/mi−WW 2
144.8 Kilometers−1.5 m/km

Dry Bay

AA

CAUTION
Attempting the Alsek River
should not be
considered lightly.

ALASKA
BRITISH COLUMBIA

UNITED STATES
CANADA

Tatshenshini River

Alsek

AA

Portage

AA

Tweedsmuir Glacier

BRITISH COLUMBIA
YUKON TERRITORY

140 Miles−20 ft/mi−WW4
225.3 Kilometers−3.8 m/km

River

Kaskawulsh River

To Haines, AK

AA
AR

Dezadeash River

Haines Highway

20 Miles
20 Kilometers

Haines Junction

To Alaska

To Whitehorse, YT

Alaska Highway

See page 58 for explanation of symbols.

㊾52

Stikine River

A link between the Pacific Ocean and Interior British Columbia is provided by the Stikine River, which rises in the Cassiar Mountains, then cuts through the magnificent mountains of the coastal range. Since ancient times man has used this route to trade, make war or search for riches and adventure. Navigation is possible as far up the river as Telegraph Creek, so called from the days when there was thought of laying an overland telegraph line from the North American continent to Europe by way of Alaska and Siberia. The silt-laden river poses no serious obstacle to the experienced river traveler, although there are fast water and rapids to negotiate around the many sand bars, shoals and narrows. Small-boat travelers should arrange for a lift across the tidal flats to Wrangell.

River Location

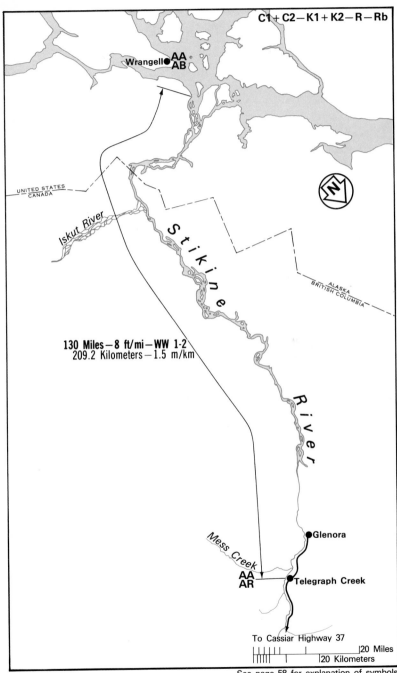

C1 + C2 — K1 + K2 — R — Rb

Wrangell AA AB

UNITED STATES
CANADA

Iskut River

S t i k i n e

ALASKA
BRITISH COLUMBIA

130 Miles — 8 ft/mi — WW 1-2
209.2 Kilometers — 1.5 m/km

R i v e r

Mess Creek

●Glenora

AA
AR

●Telegraph Creek

To Cassiar Highway 37

20 Miles
20 Kilometers

See page 58 for explanation of symbols.

⑤³ Taku River

Although its course is about 100 miles long, the Taku flows only some dozen miles from the Canadian border through Alaska before entering tidewater. The Taku's headwaters, the Inklin and Nakina rivers, are clear-water streams and major salmon-spawning areas. Streams cascading down steep, narrow, heavily timbered valleys drain the Coast Mountains to the Taku. Because of cutbanks and numerous uprooted trees that form dangerous logjams and countless sweepers, the Taku is not safe for paddling above the Tulsequah River in Canada. Riverboats can ascend the Taku as far as the Nakina River and then can continue on the Nakina for some miles, until the water becomes too swift and shallow. In former times the Indians used the Taku as an artery to the Interior, as burial sites still testify.

River Location

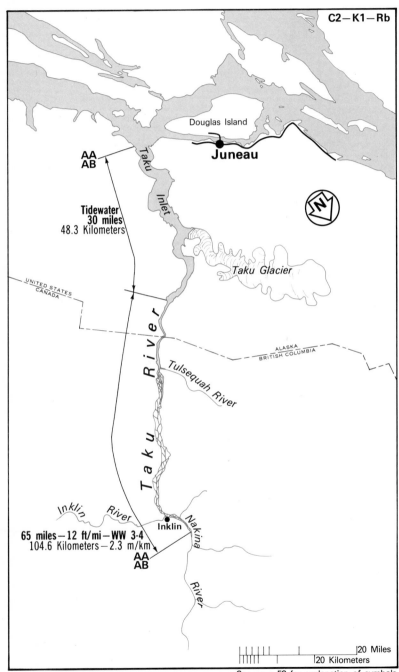

C2—K1—Rb

Douglas Island

Juneau

AA
AB

Tidewater
30 miles
48.3 Kilometers

Taku

Inlet

N

Taku Glacier

UNITED STATES
CANADA

Taku River

ALASKA
BRITISH COLUMBIA

Tulsequah River

Inklin River

Nakina

65 miles—12 ft/mi—WW 3-4
104.6 Kilometers—2.3 m/km
AA
AB

Inklin

River

20 Miles

20 Kilometers

See page 58 for explanation of symbols.

Index

Alagnak River, 102
Alatna River, 156
Alsek River, 162; character of, 6, 9;
  history of exploration of, 18;
  navigability of, 19
Ambler River, 154
Anaktuvuk River, 136; account of
  trip, 16
Aniak River, 116; chronicle of trip,
  29-33; photographs of, 28, 31, 32
Aniuk River, 142; photographs of,
  iv, 46

barge, as means to reaching starting
  point, 49
bears, confrontations with, 29, 32
Bell River, as early transportation
  route, 18; as part of Porcupine
  trip, 34
breakup, on Copper River, 40

campsites, photographic description of,
  12-13
canoes, classification of, 59; description
  of, 47; handmade, 17; transporting
  by air, 49
Chandalar River, 138
Chilikadrotna River, 118; chronicle of
  trip, 42-43; photograph of, *vi*
Chitina River, 100
Chulitna River, 76
Colville River, 146
Copper River, Chugach Range, 90;
  chronicle of trip, 38; early exploration
  of, 15; photographs of, 39, 40, 41
Copper River, Aleutian Range, 106
craft, classifications of, 59; importance
  of tying up at bank, 27; types of, 46
Cutler River, 152

damages, photographs of, 48; repairing
  of kayaks, 49
Delta River, 68; early exploration of, 15
Devil Canyon, hydroelectric
  development at, 10
difficulty of rivers, gradient as a factor,
  56; photographic summary of, 52;
  reconnoitering on foot, 55; standard
  grading system of, 57
distance, length of day's travel, 54

East Fork Sixmile Creek, 64
equipment, craft, 46; essential, 49;
  optional, 49
exploration of rivers, by Americans, 15;
  by Natives, 14; by Russians, 14-15;
  first significant thrusts, 14; in
  Interior Alaska, 14

flooding, on Aniak, 29; time of yearly
  occurrences, 49
Flora Creek, cover photograph
Fortymile River, 62

grading system, making own judgments
  in connection with, 58; of flat water,
  57, 59; of white water, 57; standard,
  57
Granite Creek, 64
Gulkana River, 88

Holitna River, 110
hydroelectric power, development of, 10

John River, 132

Kahiltna River, 78
Kantishna River, 158
kayaks, classification of, 59; description
  of, 47; handmade by youth, 19;
  photograph of, 46; transporting by
  air, 49
Killik River, 144
Klutina River, 94
Kobuk River, 150; early exploration of,
  15; general location of, 6, 7

Koyukuk River, 130; early exploration of, 15; general location of, 6, 7
Kuskokwim River, 108; early exploration of, 15; general location of, 6, 8

Little Bell River, account of trip, 34; photograph of, 35
Little Susitna River, 86
Lyon Creek, 64

Maclaren River, 72
Midas Creek, route used by Natives, 25
Miles Lake, 40
Mulchatna River, 122

Nabesna River, 92
Natives, photograph of hunting from kayaks, 14; travel routes, 16; use of rivers, 16
navigability, general of wild rivers in Alaska, 5
Nenana River, 66
Nigu River, 140; photographs of, title page, 59
Noatak River, 148; chronicle of trip, 22; drainage area of, 6, 7
Nushagak River, 120; early exploration of, 15
Nuyakuk River, 124

Old Crow, visit to, 36

paddling, average day's travel, 54; skill required, 50-51
planning voyage, predeparture activities, 46; types of craft, 46
Porcupine River, 126; account of trip, 18; as early transportation route, 18; chronicle of trip, 34; general location of, 6, 7; photograph of, 37

rafts, classification of, 59; descriptions of, 46
Redstone River, 152
riverboats, classifications of, 59
rivers (see individual names of)

safety, required equipment, 49; U.S. Coast Guard regulations, 59
Sheenjek River, 128
Sixmile Creek, 64
Skwentna River, 84
springs, mountain hot, 16
Stikine River, 164; general location of, 6, 9
Stony River, 112
Susitna River, general location of, 6, 8; lower, 82; photograph of, 2; upper, 70
sweepers, dangers of, 30

Takotna River, early exploration of, 15
Taku River, 166; general location of, 6, 9
Tanana River, 160; early exploration of, 15; general location of, 6, 8
Tazlina River, 98
Tikchik River, 114; frontispiece photograph
Togiak River, 104
Tokositna River, 76
Tonsina River, 96
topographic maps, mail-order address for, 58, 61; use and importance of, 46, 61
transportation, canoes by air, 49; getting to river, 49; rigid kayaks by air, 49
Tyone River, 74

Wild River, 134
wild rivers, definition of, 4; navigability of, 5; use today, 10
Wild and Scenic Rivers System, inclusion of Alaskan rivers in, 11

Yentna River, 80
Yukon River, drainage area of, 6, 7, 8; early exploration of, 15; historic trade route of, 16